Vegetarian Times

COMPLETE THANKSGIVING COOKBOOK

Vegetarian Times
COMPLETE
Thanksgiving
COOKBOOK

FROM THE EDITORS OF *Vegetarian Times*

MACMILLAN • USA

MACMILLAN
A Simon & Schuster Macmillan Company
1633 Broadway
New York, NY 10019

Macmillan Publishing books may be purchased for business or sales promotional use. For information please write: Special Markets Department, Macmillan Publishing USA, 1633 Broadway, New York, NY 10019.

Library of Congress Cataloging-in-Publication Data
Vegetarian times complete Thanksgiving cookbook / from the editors of
    Vegetarian times.
       p.   cm.
    Includes index.
    ISBN 0-02-862567-6 (alk. paper)
     1. Vegetarian cookery.   2. Thanksgiving cookery.   I. Vegetarian times.
  TX837.V42697   1998
  641.5'636—dc21   98-17223
                                                   CIP

Manufactured in the United States of America

10 9 8 7 6 5 4 3 2 1

Book design by designLab, Seattle, and Scott Meola

CONTENTS

Acknowledgments VII

Introduction IX

Hosting the Thanksgiving Dinner I

Tempting Appetizers..9

Raise a Glass: Delightful Beverages 29

Savory Autumn Soups 37

Salubrious Salads 51

Magnificent Entrees 67

A Harvest of Side Dishes III

Great Gravies and Table Sauces...............................149

From the Hearth: Breads, Biscuits and Muffins 157

Happy Endings: Delicious Desserts 189

Let's Feast: Thanksgiving Dinner Menus....................213

Index 219

ACKNOWLEDGMENTS

It is appropriate to take a moment in this book to give thanks to those who contributed to it. The editors of *Vegetarian Times* would like to thank Jay Solomon for authoring much of this book. His introduction reminds us all what the Thanksgiving holiday is about and his enticing chapter introductions and menus make us eager to start preparing a feast—for all the senses. Jay has worked on many of our book projects and once again has proven to be a great resource and a pleasure to work with.

Thanks also go to Janet Blake for her time researching and selecting these great Thanksgiving recipes and for her tireless perfection in copyediting them. Always a joy to work with, this is Janet's first book project for *Vegetarian Times*.

Finally, we give thanks for all of the fabulous recipe developers who have given their time and talents to create these recipes over the years. Working on a recipe takes incredible dedication and determination to "get it right." At *Vegetarian Times*, we are indeed lucky to have readers who are deeply involved in making vegetarian recipes taste great, worthy of celebrations like the ones in this book. And, we are fortunate to work with some of the best professional recipe developers and food writers in the business. Without our readers and our writers, this book would not have been possible.

Happy Thanksgiving!
—Kristen Riggs Thudium
Special Projects Manager
Vegetarian Times

INTRODUCTION

Thanksgiving is one of the most treasured American holidays. All across the country, families and friends gather for a memorable day of feasts, parades, football games and old-fashioned visiting and reminiscing. Norman Rockwell's rosy America comes alive and the fast-paced high-tech world grinds to a halt. The air is filled with excitement, camaraderie and hoopla, as well as reflection and retrospection.

The Thanksgiving holiday is steeped in tradition. It dates to around 1620, when the Pilgrims sat down with the Native Americans to celebrate the autumn harvest. Over the years, the ritual evolved into an annual observance, and in the fall of 1789, George Washington proclaimed a national day of thanksgiving. In the midst of the Civil War, President Lincoln declared the last Thursday of November the official thanksgiving holiday, and this day has been celebrated ever since. The Macy's Thanksgiving Day parade was launched in 1924, and for generations Thanksgiving has been an American institution.

From the beginning, Thanksgiving has revolved around the dinner table. Legend has it that the early gatherings celebrated the foods of the harvest season—winter squash, pumpkin, corn, wild greens, beans and cranberries. The bountiful spreads most likely included a sampling of wild fish and native fowl. At some point in the evolution of the holiday, the turkey became enshrined as the symbol and centerpiece of Thanksgiving—much to the chagrin of vegetarians!

For obvious reasons, the traditional Thanksgiving turkey dinner has presented a problem for legions of vegetarians. The annual question is: What is there to eat? For many, skipping the turkey and dining on a smörgasbord of cranberry relish, potatoes, squash, and of course, pies has been the answer. Mainstream cookbooks and magazines have typically failed to address the culinary possibilities of a meatless holiday. Consequently, on this festive gastronomic day, while most others gorged, vegetarians historically nibbled.

Thankfully, those autumn days of discontent are about to disappear forever. With the *Vegetarian Times Thanksgiving Cookbook,* it is possible to celebrate Thanksgiving without serving a shred of turkey, ham or red meat. Autumn vegetables, pumpkin, squash, cranberries, grains and beans inspire a cornucopia of new and updated dishes perfect for the holiday menu. These meatless recipes combine the staples of early gatherings with the spices and herbs of the modern pantry. With a little culinary ingenuity and moxie, the dream of preparing a magnificent vegetarian Thanksgiving feast is not just feasible but easily achievable.

The *Vegetarian Times Thanksgiving Cookbook* features the gamut of enticing preparations, from alluring appetizers, savory soups and salubrious salads to impressive main courses, an entourage of side dishes and wholesome gravies. In addition, there are tantalizing recipes for desserts, breads and beverages that are sure to bring a sense of warmth and festivity to the Thanksgiving table. Non-vegetarians, too, will discover an unexpected bonus of serving a vegetarian feast: You and your guests will not suffer from the usual post-dinner lethargy following consumption of a large meat-based meal.

Thanksgiving is many things to many people—a joyous reunion of family and friends, an opportunity to reflect and give thanks—and now, for nonvegetarians and vegetarians alike, it can be a satisfying culinary celebration. At long last, vegetarians need not endure a holiday grazing on cole slaw, macaroni salad and candied yams. The *Vegetarian Times Thanksgiving Cookbook* makes it possible to enjoy gourmet holiday fare prepared with exuberance and flair. Welcome to the bold and exciting new world of meatless holiday dining.

HOSTING
the Thanksgiving Dinner

Thanksgiving is one of the most antici-
pated gatherings of the year. It is a holiday brimming with excitement and high
expectations. For both vegetarian and nonvegetarian hosts, it is a busy and sometimes intimidating prospect. If you haven't hosted a totally vegetarian Thanksgiving
before, and you cringe at the thought of setting a turkeyless table and hearing what
Uncle Oscar will say (especially after he's had a couple of drinks), then fret no
more. With a little homework and a lot of groundwork, hosting a vegetarian
holiday meal can be an extremely rewarding and pleasurable endeavor.

There are three keys to creating any successful Thanksgiving feast: planning, preparation and presentation. This is as true for a vegetarian celebration as
for a traditional turkey dinner, but if we had only one important suggestion to
impart, it would be this: Don't let your vegetarian dinner be a surprise to your
guests on Thanksgiving Day. Neither should you apologize for it—in fact, the pos-
itive face you put on this dinner will go a long way toward convincing others that
this will be a celebration full of fun and expectation. If this is your first vegetarian

Thanksgiving, when you invite guests, tell them that you've changed the menu to a meat-free or vegetarian one and give your reasons. Let them know you've researched the options and are very excited about the dinner and the way it will be received. You might have to build some support from those family members or friends whom you know will be receptive to the idea.

You have several options for planning the meal. You can present a totally vegetarian meal and prepare every item yourself. However, most hosts encourage others to bring dishes, some based on years of tradition. Should you go this route, you must decide whether to ask your guests to make their recipes vegetarian, too (no bacon in Aunt Gretchen's green beans, no marshmallows on Uncle Harry's sweet potatoes). If not every dish is vegetarian, put a place card by those that are so your vegetarian guests won't have to question whether any dish has meat.

If you are planning a partially vegetarian meal based on a request by one or more of your guests, you can simply prepare any of the marvelous dishes in this book, including an alternative entree, for your vegetarian guests. We suggest that you inform your guests before they arrive that you will be serving a vegetarian-friendly meal, but that you will be serving turkey, too. If you are hosting a traditional meal and have requests for vegetarian options, feel free to ask your vegetarian guests to help you plan the menu and encourage them to assume the task of preparing some vegetarian dishes. Don't be surprised if those dishes are extremely popular!

No matter what level of vegetarian meal you are serving, start the ball rolling by choosing the menu, assembling shopping lists and organizing various tasks. This is when you decide what others should bring and start informing your guests that this will be a vegetarian meal. The next step, preparing the meal, means rolling up your sleeves, delving into the kitchen and bringing your grandiose plans to fruition. As with any major meal where your culinary reputation will be on the line, we suggest testing the major dishes a few weeks beforehand to see if you like them and if you think your friends and family will too. Try mixing some new dishes with some old favorites if you expect resistance. Finally, the dinner presentation is the fun part—the icing on the cake, so to speak. If you make a grand meal, you'll want to set the right mood and serve it in a proper fashion.

PLANNING THE HOLIDAY DINNER

Proper planning is the trademark of a memorable Thanksgiving feast. This stage involves browsing through recipes, deciding on a menu, envisioning the meal and compiling a shopping list. Planning and taking care of small details—such as shopping ahead of time for pantry staples or buying fresh vegetables and fruits one or two days before Thanksgiving—can make a big difference in the long run. The planning phase is often taken for granted, but without it, the potential for chaos lurks around the corner.

Here are some basic planning tips: About one week before Thanksgiving, take an inventory of the dining room and place settings. Examine your dinnerware, silverware, glasses, dessert dishes and soup bowls. Are there enough? Check out your kitchen utensils, serving spoons and pots and pans as well. This is also the time to decide on a tablecloth and centerpiece. Since you will not be putting a turkey in the center of the table, plan ahead to have an appropriate centerpiece of flowers or seasonal fruits and vegetables. Leaving the center of the table empty will just draw attention to what isn't there. Make sure there are more than enough eating utensils and dishes—you never know when unexpected friends or family members might stop by for an impromptu visit.

When planning the menu, take extra time to peruse the recipes. In this aspect, the *Vegetarian Times Thanksgiving Cookbook* can serve as a valuable resource and an inspirational tool. Browse through chapters, jot down ideas and assemble a few sample menus, or pull your menu directly from the chapter on menus starting on page 213. Draw up an outline or agenda for kitchen tasks and think of ways to optimize your time spent shopping and cooking. If you start the planning stage well in advance, time will be your friend, not your enemy.

PREPARATION: BE GREAT IN ACT

To quote Shakespeare, now is the time to "be great in act as you have been in thought." The more preparation achieved in the hours and days leading up to the big dinner, the smoother the ride will be—and the greater your enjoyment. Preparation means organizing the dishes into a cooking schedule, starting some recipes and tasks in advance and preparing the meal in a timely and efficient manner.

At first glance, producing and cooking all of the food required for a lavish menu may seem overwhelming. Early on, it is not uncommon to feel like hyperventilating at the mere thought of Thanksgiving, let alone preparing several dishes with which you are unfamiliar. However, many kitchen tasks, such as peeling, chopping, dicing and so forth, can be done in the day or two leading up to Thanksgiving. For example, soups and stews can be cooked and refrigerated; vinaigrettes and dips can be blended and chilled; desserts can be baked. You can also chill the wines and cold beverages well ahead of time. When it comes to preparation, time is on your side.

On the morning of Thanksgiving, salad greens and raw vegetables can be washed and crisped in the refrigerator. The dining room can be readied, place settings arranged and tables and chairs set up. Sweet breads and muffins can be baked; soups can be reheated. About 30 minutes before dinnertime, set out the appetizers and dips, finish the dishes that are still "works-in-progress," assemble any garnishes and make last-minute touches.

One linchpin of the preparation stage includes organizing the recipes into a checklist of kitchen duties. In addition to maximizing your time, a checklist will help ensure hot foods come out hot and cold foods come out cold. Timing is key—you'll want the hot dishes to finish at the same time. If there is a dish about which you have reservations, or if you are unsure about the length of cooking time needed, it is a good idea to test it a week or two beforehand. If you have made a dish before, most likely you will make it faster the second time around.

You will soon discover that all of this advance preparation is a great antidote to stress and anxiety, as well as contributing to a triumphant Thanksgiving dinner. Working hard—and working strategically—will be duly rewarded. Here is a checklist for your Thanksgiving preparations:

The week before Thanksgiving

Plan the menu and assemble recipes.

Take an inventory of pantry staples.

Take an inventory of dinnerware, silverware and glassware.

Make a shopping list for all foodstuffs, beverages and centerpiece, and . . .

Shop for ingredients.

One to two days before Thanksgiving

Prepare dishes that can be made ahead of time.

Make a checklist for dinner preparation and other activities.

Thanksgiving Day

Set the table well ahead of time; arrange the centerpiece.

Serve the food attractively with garnish.

Take care of last-minute details, such as lighting a fire in the fireplace, turning on music and lighting candles on the table.

Did you serve every dish that was prepared ahead of time?
(Check the fridge.)

PRESENTATION: THE MOMENT ARRIVES

Hosting a Thanksgiving feast involves more than ringing a bell, placing the food on the table and gritting your teeth. To properly present the dinner, it is important to set an upbeat mood and encourage a warm atmosphere. Paying attention to the minor details, such as decorating the room with colorful gourds and Indian corn or filling the air with soothing scents, can make a big difference. Don't forget to light the candles and turn on appropriate background music.

Proper presentation also entails serving the food in a timely manner and graceful style. After the guests are seated at the table, let the dinner unfold. The first course, such as the soup or salad and bread, starts the meal; it is followed by the main dish and entourage of side dishes, gravies and sauces. During the meal, attend to your guests' needs, but do not fuss. (Thanksgiving is traditionally a casual affair.) Sit down at the table and enjoy the meal with everyone else. Relax!

When everyone has finished the main course, clear the dishes and offer a choice of beverages (such as coffee, tea or aperitifs). As with most large meals, there should be a brief interlude before serving dessert. Remember to bring out the dessert with new silverware, and if the mood warrants, adjourn to another room. Also, pause and take a moment to enjoy the festivities before they are over.

The art of holiday entertaining can be enjoyable, satisfying, and yes, even a little challenging. With that in mind, the *Vegetarian Times Thanksgiving Cookbook* will prove to be a valuable resource for planning, preparing and serving a fabulous vegetarian dinner. With this book as a culinary blueprint, your Thanksgiving celebration can be a rousing success. Follow the lead, peruse the recipes, plan, organize, produce the meal and just watch: Good things—and good times—are bound to happen.

GUEST MANNERS COUNT

A word about being a vegetarian guest at a nonvegetarian Thanksgiving meal. True, many vegetarians have been relegated to eating a measly green salad and perhaps a few mashed potatoes at Thanksgiving, and they have put up with endless teasing and been subjected to well-meaning but uninformed hosts who tell them that the oyster stuffing is vegetarian. However, the times really are changing and as a vegetarian guest, you often have several options. Good manners go a long way, especially at a meal where relatives are assembled with whom you might or might not choose to spend a day. Our advice is not to be a victim: to take matters into your own hands and either host the meal yourself or be generous in your contributions to the meal that is being hosted by someone else. Here are some dos and don'ts that we suggest:

Do tell your host at least a month beforehand that you are vegetarian. Explain what that means to you and what you can and can't eat.

Do offer—genuinely—to help your host prepare some vegetarian selections. Offer to prepare a meatless alternative as an entree.

Do help with the menu planning and offer consultation on what is and what is not a vegetarian dish. But do so in a pleasant manner—lectures on animal cruelty are not appropriate for you to deliver to your host (unless you are asked).

Don't make a big deal about the "dead bird" in the center of the table. You are the guest; act like one.

Don't expect your host to make two different meals. But feel free to make suggestions on how some dishes can easily be made vegetarian— vegetable stock in place of chicken stock for the squash soup, a baking dish of vegetarian stuffing prepared on the side.

Don't make a big deal about what you are eating or not eating. Unless someone asks, assume no one cares.

Don't be shy about why you are a vegetarian. Share your knowledge with others when asked. But as a guest, it would be improper to proselytize at someone else's party, just as it would be at your own home as host.

Do be flexible. If you were expecting a three-course vegetarian feast and you're stuck with iceberg lettuce and overcooked green beans, don't embarrass your host. Eat what you can and focus on the conversation, the friendships and the lasting family relationships that are the biggest part of the day. Your actions and tone will reflect on all vegetarians, and there is no replacement for grace and style. Feel free to not accept your host's invitation next year, but don't make him or her miserable this year.

TEMPTING
Appetizers

Thanksgiving appetizers are the prelude to the main attraction, the opening act to the big show. As kitchen aromas gently waft throughout the house, mingling guests will seek to whet their taste buds with a light bite or little nibble. A tray of hors d'oeuvres will pique their palates and arouse their curiosity (without unduly taxing their appetites). Artful appetizers set a promising tone for the festive meal ahead.

This chapter features a variety of small dishes that radiate big flavor. There are recipes for every mood and theme, from elegant Mushroom Crostini and Autumn Tomato Bruschetta to wholesome Mock Meatballs and Lentil-and-Feta Loaf. This collection will help you begin your feast with gourmet flair, while providing a warm and tasty welcome for your guests.

When planning the Thanksgiving menu, it is a good idea to choose appetizers that can be prepared ahead of time, perhaps the day before, and then warmed up and served minutes before guests arrive. If the plan is for your guests to mingle before sitting down at the table, offer appetizers that can be eaten casually (out of hand). Also, remember that the appetizer course precedes one of the grandest dinners of the year. So, unless you are preparing an epic gastronomic spread for the ages, one or two appetizers should aptly fill the bill. As you will see, there will be plenty of opportunity to indulge later in the meal!

Avocado Dip

Try this dip with bell pepper rings, celery and fennel sticks, radishes, or broccoli and cauliflower florets.

MAKES 3½ CUPS
(56 TABLESPOONS)

½ pound soft tofu
4 avocados, pitted
3 cloves garlic, minced
2 tablespoons soy sauce
Juice from 1 lemon
Soymilk as needed

Blend together all ingredients except soymilk. Thin mixture with soymilk if too thick. Place in a serving bowl.

 Per Tablespoon: 25 Calories; 1g Protein; 2g Fat; 1g Carbohydrate; 0mg Cholesterol; 39mg Sodium; 1g Fiber.

Mock Meatballs

This hors d'oeuvre will please meat-eaters and vegetarians alike.

MAKES 24 MEATBALLS

2 cups cooked bulgur, drained
1 tablespoon minced onion
2 eggs, beaten
1 cup fresh whole-wheat bread crumbs
Oregano to taste
Freshly ground black pepper to taste
1 to 3 tablespoons olive oil
1 cup tomato juice (plus extra if needed)

Mix together bulgur, onion, eggs and bread crumbs. Season with oregano and pepper. Form mixture into walnut-sized balls.

Lightly coat a large frying pan with oil and place over medium-high heat. Add balls and cook until brown on all sides. Add tomato juice, cover pan and simmer for 5 minutes. (Add extra juice if pan is dry.) Serve in a shallow serving dish with cocktail forks or toothpicks.

Per Meatball: 32 Calories; 1g Protein; 1g Fat; 4g Carbohydrates; 18mg Cholesterol; 56mg Sodium; 1g Fiber.

Roasted Garlic Cheese Rounds
with Warm Tomato Sauce

This savory dish is a winning garlic recipe. It uses two heads of roasted garlic.

MAKES 24 SERVINGS

CRUST
3 cups water
½ teaspoon salt
1 cup uncooked polenta
1 tablespoon butter
½ teaspoon dried thyme

FILLING
3 cups chopped sweet onions, such as Maui or Vidalia
3 tablespoons butter
Two 8-ounce packages cream cheese, room temperature
1 cup ricotta cheese
1 teaspoon salt
⅛ to ¼ teaspoon cayenne pepper
2 heads roasted garlic, cooled, cloves separated and skins removed (see Note)
5 eggs
1½ cups Warm Tomato Sauce as needed (recipe follows)

To make the crust, bring water to a boil; stir in salt. Stirring constantly, drizzle polenta into boiling water. Reduce heat to low; stir in butter and thyme. Cook, stirring constantly, until polenta thickens and pulls away from sides of pan and tastes cooked, about 20 minutes. Pour polenta into an oiled, 10-inch springform pan. Spread evenly over bottom with spoon. (Dipping spoon frequently in cold water makes spreading easier.) Set aside.

To make the filling, in a nonstick frying pan, sauté onions in butter over low heat, stirring until golden brown, about 25 minutes. Cool and set aside.

Preheat oven to 350°F. With an electric mixer (do not use blender or food processor), beat together cream cheese, ricotta, salt and cayenne. Beat in roasted garlic and onions. Beat in eggs one at a time. Pour mixture into prepared pan and bake 1 hour. Turn oven off; let cheese round sit in oven 15 minutes. Remove from oven and let sit 1 hour. Serve sliced with sauce.

NOTE: *To roast garlic, remove papery outer skin from bulbs, leaving bulbs intact. Arrange bulbs in a small baking dish. Drizzle with olive oil and sprinkle with salt to taste. Bake, covered, at 350°F until garlic is soft, about 1¼ hours. When cool enough to handle, separate cloves, then squeeze cloves out of skins.*

VARIATION: *For a Mexican-style cheese round, use oregano instead of thyme in crust, and add seeded, chopped jalapeño chiles to sauce along with onion, then add 1 teaspoon cumin. After sauce has cooked, add ¼ cup chopped fresh cilantro.*

🌿 Per Serving (1 Slice with 1 Tablespoon Sauce): 146 Calories; 5g Protein; 11g Fat; 7g Carbohydrates; 74mg Cholesterol; 295mg Sodium; 1g Fiber.

Warm Tomato Sauce

This recipe makes extra sauce that can be used as a pasta topper or for lasagna. It also freezes well. If you prefer to make a smaller quantity, simply cut the recipe in half.

MAKES 16 SERVINGS
(8 CUPS)

1 cup chopped onion
3 tablespoons olive oil
Two 28-ounce cans crushed tomatoes with juice or equivalent peeled,
    seeded, diced fresh tomatoes in season
1 teaspoon onion powder
½ to 1 teaspoon garlic powder
Salt and freshly ground black pepper to taste

In a large sauté pan, cook onion in oil over medium heat until translucent, about 5 minutes. Stir in tomatoes and onion and garlic powders. Season with salt and pepper. Simmer until flavors meld, about 1 hour.

🌿 Per Serving: 64 Calories; 0g Protein; 0g Fat; 16g Carbohydrates; 0mg Cholesterol; 200mg Sodium; 0g Fiber.

Endive Spears

The classic French combination of garlic and goat cheese, here stuffed in endive, is equally good spread on toasted, sliced French bread or a baguette.

MAKES 12 SPEARS

1 head garlic, separated into cloves, but not peeled
4-ounce log goat cheese (chèvre), softened
¼ teaspoon freshly ground black pepper
2 small heads Belgian endive, separated into 12 spears
Fresh thyme or basil sprigs (optional)

Preheat oven to 400°F. Wrap garlic cloves in aluminum foil. Bake 30 minutes or until tender; cool. Squeeze pulp from peels; discard peels. In a medium bowl, combine garlic, goat cheese and pepper; mix well with fork. (At this point, mixture can be covered and refrigerated up to 48 hours before serving. Let stand at room temperature until softened.)

Spoon about 2 teaspoons cheese mixture into center of each endive spear; arrange on a colorful serving platter. Garnish with thyme or basil sprigs if using.

Per Spear: 40 Calories; 2g Protein; 3g Fat; 2g Carbohydrates; 7mg Cholesterol; 51mg Sodium; 0g Fiber.

Stuffed Mushrooms

This recipe makes delicious hors d'oeuvres. You might want to double the recipe if you're expecting a big crowd.

8 large mushrooms, about 2 inches across
3 tablespoons olive oil
¾ pound tomatoes, peeled and finely chopped (about 2 cups chopped)
1 clove garlic, crushed
1 bunch scallions, thinly sliced
3 tablespoons chopped fresh chives (or 2 teaspoons dried)
Salt and freshly ground black pepper to taste
½ teaspoon fresh lemon juice

Preheat oven to 350°F. Wipe mushrooms clean. Remove stems. Lightly oil a baking sheet with 2 teaspoons oil and lay mushrooms on it, stalk side up. Pour ½ teaspoon of oil over each one and bake 20 minutes. Let cool.

Combine tomatoes, garlic and scallions on a chopping board and chop until reduced to a puree. (Or process in a food processor for a few seconds, being careful not to overprocess.) Put mixture in a bowl and stir in chives, salt and pepper. Stir in remaining 1 tablespoon olive oil and lemon juice. Fill each mushroom cap with mixture.

Per Serving: 126 Calories; 2g Protein; 11g Fat; 8g Carbohydrates; 0mg Cholesterol; 12mg Sodium; 2g Fiber.

Mixed Olives with Herbs

This appetizer of black and green olives is as pretty as beach stones. Spoon them into decorative bowls for guests to nibble on.

MAKES 6 SERVINGS
(2 CUPS)

2 cups mixed green and black pitted olives (such as Kalamata, Niçoise,
    or Sicilian)
10 sprigs fresh thyme
4 bay leaves
1 large clove garlic, thinly sliced
$1/4$ teaspoon fennel seeds
Several strips orange peel
2 tablespoons extra-virgin olive oil

Combine all ingredients in a covered container. Refrigerate up to 4 days. Serve at room temperature.

NOTE: *If using oil-cured olives, add them just before serving, because they tend to stain the green ones black.*

Per Serving: 128 Calories; 1g Protein; 13g Fat; 5g Carbohydrates; 0mg Cholesterol; 660mg Sodium; 2g Fiber.

Orange-and-Gold Millet Terrine

The layers of pale-gold millet and pureed carrot make this elegant terrine worth the extra work. For an elegant appetizer, arrange on a bed of lettuce and serve with crackers.

MAKES 8 SERVINGS

3 cups sliced carrots
$\frac{1}{2}$ teaspoon ground cardamom
1 tablespoon honey
1 teaspoon vegetable oil
$\frac{1}{4}$ cup white wine or vegetable broth
2 green onions, chopped
$\frac{1}{2}$ cup minced onion
2 cups chopped mushrooms
3 cloves garlic, minced
$\frac{1}{4}$ teaspoon ground coriander
$\frac{1}{4}$ teaspoon dried basil
$\frac{1}{2}$ teaspoon dried thyme
3 cups cooked millet
2 eggs (or equivalent Egg Replacer), lightly beaten
$\frac{1}{2}$ cup chopped fresh parsley
$\frac{1}{2}$ cup plain nonfat yogurt or soy yogurt
$\frac{1}{2}$ cup soft whole-wheat bread crumbs
$1\frac{1}{2}$ teaspoons salt or herbal salt
2 tablespoons low-sodium soy sauce
$\frac{1}{4}$ teaspoon cayenne pepper
8 to 10 lettuce leaves

Preheat oven to 350°F. Lightly oil a 9-by-5-inch loaf pan. Steam carrots for 5 minutes or until soft. Drain, then puree in blender with cardamom and honey. Set aside.

In a large skillet, over medium-high heat, heat oil and wine or broth until bubbling. Add green onions and minced onion. Cook, stirring, until limp, about 3 minutes. Add mushrooms, garlic, coriander, basil and thyme. Cook, stirring, until mushrooms exude moisture, about 5 minutes. Remove pan from heat and stir in remaining ingredients except lettuce. Mix well.

Spread half of carrot puree into the bottom of the prepared loaf pan, smoothing with a spoon. Top with all the millet mixture, again smoothing the layer. Then spread on remaining carrot puree. Place loaf pan in a 9-by-13-inch shallow baking dish. Add 1 inch of water to baking dish (the steaming water will prevent pâté from browning as it cooks). Bake 1 hour, or until firm. Cut into 1-inch slices and serve on lettuce.

Per Serving: 195 Calories; 7g Protein; 3g Fat; 35g Carbohydrates; 47mg Cholesterol; 651mg Sodium; 4g Fiber.

Spinach-Cheese Twists

This recipe, by *Vegetarian Times* reader Christine Vidra of Maumee, Ohio, won a reader contest. It can be served as an appetizer or as a bread.

Dough
16-ounce package hot roll mix
1 cup part-skim ricotta cheese
²/₃ cup hot water
1 egg
Flour for rolling dough

Filling
2 tablespoons margarine or butter
1 clove garlic, minced
1 teaspoon dried basil
¹/₂ teaspoon onion powder
9-ounce package frozen spinach, thawed and squeezed to drain
¹/₄ cup freshly grated Parmesan cheese

Topping
1 egg white
2 teaspoons water
1 tablespoon freshly grated Parmesan cheese

Lightly grease a 9- or 10-inch springform pan with nonstick cooking spray or oil. In a large bowl, combine hot roll mix with yeast from foil packet included in the package; mix well. Stir in ricotta cheese, water and egg until dough pulls away from the sides of bowl. Turn dough out onto a lightly floured surface.

With greased or floured hands, shape dough into a ball. Knead dough for 5 minutes until smooth. If desired, sprinkle additional flour over surface to reduce stickiness. Cover ball with a large bowl; let rest 5 minutes.

Melt margarine or butter in a small saucepan over medium-high heat. Stir in garlic, basil and onion powder. Cook and stir 1 minute. Set aside.

In a small bowl, combine spinach and ¹/₄ cup Parmesan cheese. Mix well. Return to dough and gently punch down several times to remove all air bubbles. On a lightly floured surface, roll out dough to a 15-by-18-inch rectangle. Spread with margarine mixture to within 1 inch of edges. Spoon spinach mixture evenly over dough to within 1 inch of edges.

Starting with 18-inch side, roll dough into a cylinder. Pinch edges firmly to seal. With a sharp knife, cut roll lengthwise, forming 2 strips. With cut sides facing up, twist strips together. Form dough into circle; pinch ends together tightly to seal. Carefully place circle in greased pan. Cover loosely with greased plastic wrap and a cloth towel. Let rise in a warm place until light and doubled in size, about 20 to 35 minutes.

Preheat oven to 375°F. Uncover dough. In a small bowl, beat egg white and water. Brush over dough and sprinkle with Parmesan cheese. Bake 30 to 40 minutes, until deep golden brown. Remove from pan and let cool completely. Cut into slices.

Per Serving: 97 Calories; 5g Protein; 3g Fat; 12g Carbohydrates; 21mg Cholesterol; 173mg Sodium; 1g Fiber.

Walnut-Stuffed Baby Red Potatoes

These little red potatoes—topped with sour cream, walnuts and festive sprigs of dill—look perfect for the holidays.

MAKES 24 SERVINGS

24 baby red potatoes
¾ cup sour half-and-half or sour cream
24 walnut halves, toasted
24 sprigs fresh dill

Cook potatoes in boiling water for 8 to 12 minutes, until just tender.

Drain and cool. Slice off bottom end of each potato so it sits upright, and slice off a third of top. (If potatoes are medium-small, cut them in half and use both halves.) With a melon baller, scoop out potato and fill with a dollop of sour half-and-half or sour cream. Top with a walnut half and tuck in a sprig of dill.

HELPFUL HINT: *Potatoes can be boiled and scooped out up to 3 days in advance. Filled potatoes can be prepared up to several hours in advance, but they are best served when freshly assembled.*

Per Serving: 125 Calories; 3g Protein; 5g Fat; 19g Carbohydrates; 3mg Cholesterol; 2g Fiber.

Mushroom Crostini

Italians call these *funghi trifolati*, or "truffled mushrooms," because they are sliced thinly in the way truffles usually are.

Makes 8 servings

1 teaspoon olive oil
2 cloves garlic, minced
1 pound mushrooms, sliced very thin
Juice of 1 lemon (about 3 tablespoons)
1 loaf Italian bread
1 clove garlic
¼ cup minced fresh Italian parsley leaves

In a large nonstick skillet, heat oil. Sauté minced garlic in oil 1 minute. Add mushrooms and lemon juice; cook over medium heat until liquid has evaporated, about 10 minutes. Slice bread into ½-inch-thick slices and toast. Rub toast with remaining 1 clove garlic. Top each bread slice with mushroom mixture and sprinkle with parsley.

Per Serving: 147 Calories; 5g Protein; 2g Fat; 27g Carbohydrates; 0mg Cholesterol; 265mg Sodium; 2g Fiber.

Autumn Tomato Bruschetta

When tomatoes are out of season, roast them first to bring out their flavor.

MAKES 8 SERVINGS

4 pounds beefsteak tomatoes, fresh or roasted
1 tablespoon olive oil
1 loaf bread for crostini or other Italian bread
2 cloves garlic

To roast tomatoes, preheat oven to 500°F. Oil a 9-by-12-inch baking dish. Slice tomatoes in ½-inch-thick slices, then cut slices in half, or in quarters if very large.

Layer tomato slices in baking dish. Brush each layer with oil. Roast tomatoes until very soft, about 4 to 5 minutes.

Meanwhile, slice bread into 1-inch slices. Place on baking sheet. Bake bread until toasted, 3 to 4 minutes; remove from oven and rub each slice with garlic clove. Remove tomatoes from pan with a slotted spoon or spatula; place on top of bread slices.

 Per Serving: 186 Calories; 6g Protein; 4g Fat; 33g Carbohydrates; 0mg Cholesterol; 160mg Sodium; 4g Fiber.

Creamy Herb Spread

The combination of reduced-fat firm tofu, mild miso and a tiny bit of sesame tahini along with herbs and garlic results in a spread or thick dip not unlike a rich herbed cream cheese.

MAKES 14 SERVINGS
(3½ CUPS)

12-ounce reduced-fat firm tofu, drained and crumbled
3 tablespoons light miso
1 tablespoon sesame tahini
1 green onion, chopped
4 tablespoons minced fresh parsley
2 teaspoons dry dill weed (2 tablespoons fresh), or other herb of choice
1 clove garlic, crushed
Pinch freshly grated nutmeg

Combine all ingredients in a food processor; pulse until smooth. Pack into a serving bowl. Serve immediately with crusty bread, crackers, breadsticks and/or raw vegetables.

HELPFUL HINT: *If you cannot find reduced-fat tofu, substitute firm tofu. The results will be similar but fat count will be slightly higher.*

Per ¼ cup Serving: 40 Calories; 4g Protein; 2g Fat; 3g Carbohydrates; 0mg Cholesterol; 136mg Sodium; 1g Fiber.

Lentil-and-Feta Loaf with Sun-Dried Tomato Catsup

This loaf is best served at room temperature; it also reheats beautifully. The slices can be cut in quarters and used as appetizers, topped with a little of the catsup (recipe follows).

MAKES 6 SERVINGS

1 teaspoon olive oil
1 teaspoon cumin seeds
1 teaspoon fennel seeds
¼ teaspoon cayenne pepper
1½ cups cooked lentils
1 cup diced red onion
1 cup cooked long-grain brown or white rice
1 tablespoon salt-reduced tomato paste
¾ cup vegetable broth
2 eggs, or 3 egg whites
1½ cups fresh bread crumbs
½ cup crumbled feta cheese

Preheat oven to 375°F. Heat oil in a large saucepan over medium-low heat. Add cumin and fennel seeds; heat until seeds are fragrant, about 1 minute. Mix in cayenne pepper, lentils, onions, rice, tomato paste and broth. Cook until no liquid remains, about 5 minutes. Cool slightly; fold in remaining ingredients. Spoon into a nonstick 9-by-3-inch loaf pan. Bake until firm, about 45 minutes.

Slice and serve with Sun-Dried Tomato Catsup if desired (recipe follows).

NOTE: *Any cheese may be used, but with feta, there is no need for additional salt. If a low-salt or other mild cheese is substituted, more salt may be needed.*

◢ Per Serving (Without Catsup): 184 Calories; 10g Protein; 7g Fat; 21g Carbohydrates; 88mg Cholesterol; 248mg Sodium; 5g Fiber.

Sun-Dried Tomato Catsup

This catsup complements the Lentil-and-Feta Loaf nicely. Make enough to have some on hand for other dishes.

MAKES 16 SERVINGS
(32 TABLESPOONS)

14-ounce natural-style tomato catsup
2 tablespoons minced fresh basil
$^1/_2$ cup minced reconstituted sun-dried tomatoes

Mix all ingredients. Store covered in the refrigerator (keeps up to 4 months).

🍃 Per Serving: 32 Calories; 0g Protein; 0g Fat; 8g Carbohydrates; 0mg Cholesterol; 385mg Sodium; 1g Fiber.

Would-You-Like-a-Bite Stuffed Portobello Mushroom

One large portobello mushroom will feed two people, so increase the recipe as needed for your Thanksgiving guests.

MAKES 2 SERVINGS

$^1/_4$ cup diced sweet onion
1 teaspoon olive oil
Pinch brown sugar
$^1/_2$ cup crumbled firm tofu, squeezed dry
Salt to taste
1 large portobello mushroom, cleaned and stem removed
Pinch freshly grated nutmeg
Herb garnish of chopped fresh mint, parsley or cilantro

Preheat oven to 350°F. Sauté onion with oil and sugar over medium-low heat until onion is soft and transparent, 4 to 5 minutes. Add tofu and salt; lightly brown tofu. Remove from heat.

Place mushroom, stem side up, on a baking sheet. Mound filling over stem side of mushroom; dust with nutmeg. Bake 10 to 15 minutes on middle oven rack. Garnish with mint, parsley or cilantro. To serve, slice into wedges.

🍃 Per Serving: 83 Calories; 6g Protein; 4g Fat; 6g Carbohydrates; 0mg Cholesterol; 294mg Sodium; 2g Fiber.

Herbed White Bean Pâté

Serve this smooth pâté as a dip or spread with whole-grain bread, crackers or vegetables.

MAKES 2½ CUPS
(40 TABLESPOONS)

½ cup peeled and diced shallots or scallions (mostly white part)
3 cloves garlic, minced, or to taste
2 cups cooked white beans
1 tablespoon lemon juice or white wine vinegar
½ teaspoon dried basil
½ teaspoon dried thyme
½ teaspoon dried dill weed
½ teaspoon dried tarragon
½ teaspoon freshly ground white pepper
¼ teaspoon freshly ground nutmeg
½ teaspoon salt or to taste

OPTIONAL INGREDIENTS
1 tablespoon capers
1 to 2 teaspoons prepared stone-ground mustard
1 tablespoon tahini or olive oil
2 tablespoons minced fresh parsley or chives
1 tablespoon minced fresh tarragon, cilantro, dill weed or basil
Dash hot pepper sauce
Watercress, fresh minced herbs, lemon slices or olives for garnish

Place shallots or scallions and garlic in a food processor or blender; process a few seconds. Add all remaining ingredients except those that are optional; puree until smooth. Taste and add optional ingredients as desired; puree until smooth. Transfer to a serving dish or decorative crock and garnish.

HELPFUL HINT: *Refrigerate overnight to allow flavors to develop.*

Per Tablespoon: 13 Calories; 1g Protein; 0g Fat; 2g Carbohydrates; 0mg Cholesterol; 30mg Sodium; 0g Fiber.

Marinated Mushrooms and Hazelnuts

Crunchy, soft, sweet and tart all at the same time, this marinated mushroom dish from the Andalusian region of Spain is anything but ordinary. Serve with forks, wooden toothpicks or bread for scooping.

Makes 6 servings

1 cup hazelnuts
$^1/_3$ cup red wine or red wine vinegar
2 tablespoons olive oil
$^1/_2$ teaspoon salt
$^1/_4$ teaspoon freshly ground black pepper
$^1/_2$ teaspoon dried thyme
$^1/_2$ teaspoon fennel seeds, slightly crushed
$^1/_2$ pound small button mushrooms, cut in half (about 3 cups)

Preheat oven to 350°F. Spread hazelnuts on a baking sheet and toast in oven until aromatic, about 10 minutes. Rub nuts with a kitchen towel to remove their papery skins. Coarsely shop nuts and set aside.

In a skillet, combine red wine or vinegar, oil, salt, pepper, thyme and fennel. Heat over low flame until barely bubbling. Do not allow to simmer. Add mushrooms and heat just until mushrooms exude a little moisture, about 5 minutes. Transfer to a bowl and add nuts. Refrigerate, covered, at least 2 hours, preferably overnight. Serve chilled or at room temperature.

VARIATION: *Substitute 1 cup blanched almonds for the hazelnuts.*

🍃 Per Serving: 271 Calories; 7g Protein; 25g Fat; 8g Carbohydrates; 0mg Cholesterol; 196mg Sodium; 6g Fiber.

RAISE A GLASS:
Delightful Beverages

Beverages are an important yet often underrated aspect of the holiday meal. Of course, food is in the spotlight, but beverages can help to cleanse the palate and heighten the overall flavors of the meal. Additionally, the Thanksgiving dinner, like other lavish feasts, is bound to include a celebratory toast or two—an occasion when the beverages briefly take center stage. A salutation may fall flat without a proper drink to raise high in unison.

Depending on your mood or disposition, it is a good idea to offer a choice of nonalcoholic and alcoholic drinks to your guests. Apple cider, sodas and sparkling waters are all welcome possibilities. When it comes to alcoholic drinks, beer and wine are both widely accepted, while Champagne and fine liqueurs add a touch of class to the festivities. As for mixed cocktails, it's a matter of personal taste and judgment. Keep in mind that most people perceive Thanksgiving as a sentimental holiday, not a boisterous happy hour.

For both large and small gatherings, providing a choice of white and red wines reveals a genuine understanding of proper hosting etiquette. As a general rule, red wines, such as cabernet sauvignon, merlot and pinot noir, will complement robustly flavored dishes, red and brown sauces and rich gravies and soups. White wines, such as chardonnay and sauvignon blanc, will complement light sauces, soups and most rice and grain dishes. Assertive wines, such as Gewürztraminer, riesling and zinfandel, are good choices to pair with spicy or aggressively seasoned dishes. If you have any questions, ask the sommelier at a local wine shop.

No matter what kind of alcohol you serve, there is one important word to keep in mind: moderation. Thanksgiving is defined as many things—a culinary celebration, a family reunion, a time to reflect—but it is not a keg party. The "American way" may be to go overboard with lavish food and luscious desserts, but when it comes to alcoholic drinks, restraint is the rule.

Rosy Mulled Cider

Cinnamon sticks and strawberries make this mulled cider a real treat.

MAKES 4 SERVINGS
(4 CUPS)

4 cups apple cider
4 cinnamon sticks
1 tablespoon honey or sugar
Juice of $^1/_2$ lemon (about $1^1/_2$ tablespoons)
$^1/_4$ cup frozen unsweetened strawberries, mashed or pureed, with juice

Combine cider, cinnamon sticks, honey or sugar and lemon juice in a medium saucepan over medium-high heat. Add strawberry puree; bring to a boil. Simmer 15 minutes. Strain and serve in glass or ceramic mugs garnished with the cinnamon sticks.

Per Serving: 145 Calories; 0g Protein; 0g Fat; 40g Carbohydrates; 0mg Cholesterol; 8mg Sodium; 0g Fiber.

Mock Champagne

All the fun without the alcohol, this drink can be made in any quantity. For pink "Champagne," use cranberry-apple sparkling cider.

MAKES 6 SERVINGS
(6 CUPS)

4 cups sparkling apple cider, chilled
2 cups tangerine- or orange-flavored sparkling water, chilled
Pinch ground ginger
Fresh strawberries for garnish

In a large pitcher, mix apple cider and sparkling water. Add ginger and mix briefly. Pour into stemmed glasses and garnish each glass with a fresh strawberry.

Per Serving: 120 Calories; 1g Protein; 0g Fat; 32g Carbohydrates; 0mg Cholesterol; 13mg Sodium; 0g Fiber.

Apple Brandy

This warming concoction is elegant and easy to toss together.

6 cloves
2 teaspoons lemon zest
2 1/2 cups apple cider
Two 2-inch cinnamon sticks
2 tablespoons brandy

In a medium saucepan, combine cloves, zest, cider and cinnamon sticks. Bring to boil, cover and simmer gently 3 to 5 minutes.

Remove from heat. Strain out zest, cloves and cinnamon. Add brandy and serve.

VARIATION: *For an alcohol-free drink, omit the brandy or use brandy-flavored extract.*

 Per Serving: 178 Calories; 0g Protein; 0g Fat; 36g Carbohydrates; 0mg Cholesterol; 9mg Sodium; 0g Fiber.

Apple Cocktail

Here's a mellow variation on a Champagne cocktail. Make it with or without the alcohol.

Angostura bitters
1 sugar cube
1 ounce Calvados and 4 ounces Champagne for alcoholic drink,
    or 5 ounces sparkling apple cider for nonalcoholic drink

Place 1 drop bitters on sugar cube; place sugar cube in serving glass. Pour in Calvados and Champagne, or sparkling apple cider. Stir gently.

Per Serving (Alcoholic): 170 Calories; 0g Protein; 0g Fat; 8g Carbohydrates; 0mg Cholesterol; 0mg Sodium; 0g Fiber.

Per Serving (Nonalcoholic): 93 Calories; 0g Protein; 0g Fat; 25g Carbohydrates; 0mg Cholesterol; 4mg Sodium; 0g Fiber.

"Champagne"

This tastes amazingly like the real thing. If you prefer pink Champagne, add a tablespoon or two of grenadine or cranberry juice.

Makes 8 servings

32-ounce bottle club soda or seltzer
Two 6-ounce cans frozen white grape juice concentrate, thawed

Stir together club soda or seltzer and grape juice concentrate. Pour into two soda bottles. Cap tightly and chill.

Per Serving: 96 Calories; 0g Protein; 0g Fat; 24g Carbohydrates; 0mg Cholesterol; 29mg Sodium; 0g Fiber.

Café Latte

This is a favorite after-dinner coffee. Almost a dessert itself!

Makes 1 large serving
or 2 smaller servings

2 tablespoons ground espresso-blend coffee
6 ounces hot (200°F) water
6 ounces milk, soymilk or nondairy creamer

Brew coffee according to coffeemaker's instructions. Steam or scald milk, soymilk or nondairy creamer according to method of choice. (See methods below.) Pour milk into a large mug or French coffee "bowl." Add coffee; top with milk.

VARIATIONS: *To basic café latte, add a shot of flavored syrup or an extract such as vanilla, orange or chocolate; ¼ teaspoon ground cinnamon, nutmeg or ginger; ⅛ teaspoon fresh lemon or orange zest; or 1 ground clove. For an alcoholic beverage, add a drop or two of anise-flavored liqueur, brandy or rum.*

Per Serving: 117 Calories; 6g Protein; 6g Fat; 9g Carbohydrates; 25mg Cholesterol; 94mg Sodium; 0g Fiber.

Per Small Serving: 59 Calories; 3g Protein; 3g Fat; 5g Carbohydrates; 13g Carbohydrates; 13g Cholesterol; 47mg Sodium; 0g Fiber.

Chai Masala

Spiced tea has as many varieties as there are Indian households. Indians enjoy chai masala as a snack, as a restorative and as a dessert. Experiment with different spice combinations until you find your "personalized" chai spices. The recipe that follows gives loose measurements, as you must brew and combine to your taste.

MAKES 2 SERVINGS AS A HOT BEVERAGE
OR 3 OVER ICE

2 tablespoons loose tea (or bags to make 2 cups of tea)
14 ounces hot (180°F) water
1 teaspoon spice mix (see Note)
6 ounces milk, soymilk or nondairy creamer

Combine tea and water; allow to steep off heat for at least 10 minutes. For stronger, darker tea, heat tea and water over low heat until desired strength is reached.

Steam or scald milk, soymilk or nondairy creamer according to method of choice. (See methods below.) Combine steeped tea, steamed or scalded milk, soymilk or nondairy creamer and spice mix in a small saucepan; heat over low heat until chai is hot, about 1 minute. Serve immediately or refrigerate and serve chilled, over ice. Chai masala is served both sweetened and unsweetened. If sweetening, use the sweetener of your choice.

NOTE: *Chai masala spice mixtures can be purchased at Indian markets, or you can make your own by mixing together equal parts ground ginger, cinnamon and cardamom. Your spice mixture will have the best flavor if you grind your own spices using a mortar and pestle or an electric coffee grinder.*

VARIATION: *Add vanilla extract or vanilla sugar to the spice mixture. To make vanilla sugar, place a vanilla bean in a tightly covered jar of sugar. Allow flavors to blend before using.*

Per Serving: 117 Calories; 6g Protein; 6g Fat; 10g Carbohydrates; 25mg Cholesterol; 104mg Sodium; 0g Fiber.

Per Cold Serving: 78 Calories; 4g Protein; 4g Fat; 7g Carbohydrates; 17mg Cholesterol; 69mg Sodium; 0g Fiber.

Three Methods

to Scald or Steam Milk

If you have a home espresso machine, follow the manufacturer's instructions for using the steam spigot to steam milk, soymilk or nondairy creamer. Traditionally, milk is heated in a metal pitcher with a spout and handle large enough to hold the expanding volume as the milk froths during steaming. Pour the steamed milk into a mug, then pour the espresso over the milk. A foamy cap of milk from the pitcher finishes the beverage.

Using the microwave method, put milk, soymilk or nondairy creamer in a container large enough to allow the liquid to expand during heating. A 1-quart glass measuring cup for 6 ounces of milk works well. Heat the milk at full power until a skin starts to form, about 2 minutes; continue to heat until the liquid under the skin looks as if it is going to break through. Remove from heat, allow to cool about 2 minutes and repeat the process. Discard the milk skin on the surface. Holding the measuring cup as high as possible, pour the milk into a coffee mug. This creates bubbles that form the foamy cap. This takes some practice but is worth the end product. Alternatively, whisk the milk before pouring to form bubbles, or whirl briefly in a blender.

Using the stovetop method, bring the milk, soymilk or nondairy creamer to a boil over medium-high heat in a container large enough to handle expansion. A quart saucepan with 6 ounces of milk works well. When milk is foamy, remove from heat. Discard the milk skin on the surface. Holding the pan as high as possible, pour the milk into a mug, whisk the milk before pouring or whirl briefly in the blender.

SAVORY
Autumn Soups

*A*utumn is the season for wholesome, good-for-you soups. Simmering, aromatic soup is a welcome prelude to the Thanksgiving feast and fills the air with a sense of anticipation and comfort. Savory soup whets the appetite, nourishes the spirit and soothes the soul. No matter how hectic the holidays can become, when a tureen of soup arrives at the table, all is well with the world.

This chapter features an array of traditional and innovative soups, chowders and bisques that are ideal for a festive autumn celebration. From Cream of Corn Soup and Mushroom Wild Rice Chowder to Potato-Pumpkin Soup and Roasted Red Pepper and Sweet Potato Soup, this bounty of soup recipes will pique your culinary curiosity and enliven almost any Thanksgiving menu. Especially with the colder, shorter days of December right around the corner, soup makes a welcome and natural first course.

From a practical standpoint, the recipes in this chapter call for widely available ingredients, are easy to prepare and can be made well ahead of time. In fact, you can cook the soup the day before, store it in the refrigerator and gradually reheat it (in a sturdy saucepan) just before dinnertime. (Most soups actually taste better after they are reheated the next day.) In addition, with the soup already finished, there might be less stress and commotion in the kitchen—a bonus for the time-challenged host whose plate is sure to be already chock-full with last-minute details.

Cream of Yam and Carrot Soup

The yams and carrots give the soup a deliciously sweet taste, and they provide a significant dose of beta-carotene as well.

MAKES 5 SERVINGS
(5 CUPS)

1 tablespoon extra-virgin olive oil
3 to 4 cloves garlic, sliced
1 medium onion, cut into big chunks
4 medium carrots, peeled and cut into chunks
1 large yam or sweet potato, peeled and cut into chunks
2 bay leaves
1 teaspoon salt, or to taste
Chopped fresh parsley or green onion tops for garnish (optional)

In a large skillet, heat oil over medium heat. Add garlic and onion and cook, stirring often, until onion is softened, about 5 minutes. Add remaining vegetables, bay leaves, salt and enough water to just cover vegetables. Bring mixture to a boil over medium-high heat. Reduce heat, cover and simmer until the carrots are soft, about 30 minutes. Discard bay leaves.

Transfer mixture to a food processor or blender and process until smooth. Adjust salt if necessary, and ladle into serving bowls. Garnish with parsley or green onions if desired.

🍃 Per Serving: 84 Calories; 1g Protein; 3g Fat; 14g Carbohydrates; 0mg Cholesterol; 489mg Sodium; 3g Fiber.

Roasted Red Pepper and Sweet Potato Soup

Sweet potatoes and roasted peppers blend into a beautiful soup—golden and creamy, with a robust but slightly sweet flavor. It makes a great starter to the Thanksgiving meal but also can be enjoyed on its own.

MAKES 8 SERVINGS
(8 CUPS)

1 tablespoon olive oil
1 large onion, peeled and chopped (2 cups)
2 cloves garlic, crushed
1½ pounds sweet potatoes, peeled and cut into ½ -inch cubes (6 cups)
6 cups vegetable stock or water
2 to 3 sprigs fresh thyme
3 large red bell peppers
2 tablespoons fresh lemon juice
Cayenne pepper to taste
Salt and freshly ground black pepper to taste
2 tablespoons sour cream for garnish
Small sprigs fresh thyme for garnish

Preheat broiler. In a large pot, heat oil over medium heat. Add onion and garlic; cover and cook over medium-low heat, until onion is soft, about 5 minutes. Add sweet potatoes and stir well; cover and cook 10 minutes. Add stock or water and thyme; bring to a boil. Reduce heat; cover and simmer until potatoes are tender, about 15 minutes.

Meanwhile, roast peppers under broiler, turning with tongs until charred all over, about 10 minutes. When peppers are cool enough to handle, remove charred skins, stem, seeds and ribs.

Discard thyme sprigs from soup. Transfer soup and roasted bell peppers to a blender or food processor and process until smooth. Return mixture to pot and gently reheat. Add lemon juice, cayenne, salt and pepper to taste.

To serve, ladle soup into warmed bowls and garnish each serving with a swirl of sour cream and several small sprigs of thyme.

Per Serving: 166 Calories; 2g Protein; 3g Fat; 34g Carbohydrates; 2mg Cholesterol; 17mg Sodium; 5g Fiber.

Potato-Mushroom Soup with Apple

This hearty autumn soup combines the earthy flavors of potatoes, mushrooms, onions and scallions. The diced apple provides a sweet, crunchy contrast to the savory broth.

MAKES 6 SERVINGS

6 scallions, sliced thinly
1 small onion, finely chopped
1½ tablespoons margarine
1 tablespoon vegetable oil
3 cups peeled and thinly sliced potatoes
1½ cups sliced mushrooms
6 cups vegetable broth
1 to 2 tablespoons soy sauce
¼ teaspoon freshly ground black pepper
½ teaspoon dried thyme
3 tablespoons chopped fresh Italian parsley
1 Rome apple, cored and finely diced

In a large saucepan, sauté scallions and onion in margarine and oil over medium-high heat for 2 minutes. Add potatoes and mushrooms, and sauté 5 minutes. Add broth, soy sauce and pepper. Cover and simmer 15 minutes, or until potatoes are tender. Add thyme and taste for seasoning. Before serving, add parsley and apple.

🍂 Per Serving: 131 Calories; 4g Protein; 4g Fat; 23g Carbohydrates; 0mg Cholesterol; 1216mg Sodium; 2g Fiber.

Cream of Corn Soup

This soup can be thick or thin, depending on whether you add the cornmeal.

1 quart water
2 cups corn kernels
1 leek, thinly sliced
1 teaspoon minced garlic (1 large clove)
1 red or green bell pepper, diced
1 teaspoon celery seed
2 teaspoons chili powder
Salt to taste
1 cup cornmeal mixed with 1 cup water (optional)
1 to 3 cups soymilk or rice milk
1 tablespoon soy sauce

In a large pot or Dutch oven, boil water. Add corn, leek, garlic, bell pepper, celery seed, chili powder and salt. Simmer 30 minutes, stirring occasionally.

For a thick soup, add cornmeal mixture gradually and simmer, stirring. Begin adding soymilk or rice milk until soup reaches desired consistency. Simmer until cornmeal is cooked, about 15 minutes. Stir in soy sauce.

For a thin soup, omit cornmeal mixture and stir in soymilk or rice milk, and soy sauce to taste. (You might need less soy sauce.)

Per Serving: 345 Calories; 10g Protein; 5g Fat; 67g Carbohydrates; 0mg Cholesterol; 241mg Sodium; 2g Fiber.

Vegetable–Wild Rice Soup

Make this soup a day or two before Thanksgiving. It's important to keep the heat adjusted so the soup remains at a lively simmer and ingredients cook in the order added.

MAKES 16 SERVINGS

4 quarts vegetable stock
3 large garlic cloves, minced
¼ cup sun-dried (not oil-packed) tomatoes, snipped into small pieces
2 large carrots, halved and sliced ⅛-inch thick
1 medium parsnip, diced
1 cup celery, thinly sliced
1 cup green beans, trimmed and chopped
2 leeks, white part only, cleaned and thinly sliced
2 cups shredded cabbage
1 cup wild rice
1 cup brown lentils, washed and picked over
4 new red potatoes, quartered
Salt and freshly ground black pepper to taste
1 cup frozen green peas
Freshly grated Parmesan cheese (optional)

In a large stockpot, bring stock to a boil. Reduce heat to a simmer; add garlic and tomatoes. Stir; bring soup back to a steady simmer.

Add ingredients in the following order, bringing soup back to a steady simmer between each addition: carrots, parsnip, celery, green beans, leeks and cabbage. After adding cabbage, simmer 25 minutes.

Add rice, lentils and potatoes all at once; simmer 35 minutes.

Add salt and black pepper. Add green peas. Cook only until soup returns to a simmer. Serve with a dish of grated Parmesan for passing at table, if desired.

HELPFUL HINT: *If liquid seems to be evaporating too fast, cover soup, reducing heat to maintain simmer.*

VARIATION: *Substitute 1 cup peeled, diced turnips for parsnip.*

🥄 Per Serving: 147 Calories; 7g Protein; 1g Fat; 30g Carbohydrates; 0mg Cholesterol; 339mg Sodium; 7g Fiber.

Chestnut Soup with Greens

Native Americans used acorns for this soup, but since they are not commercially available, we've substituted chestnuts. Canned, unsweetened chestnut puree is easy to use, as are fresh chestnuts. In Asian grocery stores you also can find dried chestnuts. These can be used by soaking overnight and then simmering until tender.

MAKES 8 SERVINGS

2 cups finely diced onion
1 pound chestnuts, roasted, peeled and ground in food processor,
    or 15$\frac{1}{2}$-ounce can unsweetened chestnut puree
6 cups water
2 teaspoons salt
1 bunch watercress, washed, stems removed
2 cups dandelion greens or arugula
1 bunch scallions, sliced (green part only)

Combine onions, chestnut puree and water in a 4-quart stockpot. Simmer 15 minutes; add salt. Just before serving, add greens and scallions; cook briefly until wilted.

VARIATIONS: *A wider variety of fresh greens may be added, but they should be very tender leaves that could be used in a salad. You also can add edible flowers.*

Per Serving: 152 Calories; 4g Protein; 1g Fat; 33g Carbohydrates; 0mg Cholesterol; 601mg Sodium; 2g Fiber.

Classic Onion Soup

Readers tells us that onion soup is one of the dishes they miss the most when they go vegetarian; here's a version without beef broth.

MAKES 6 SERVINGS

2 tablespoons margarine
2 tablespoons olive oil
4 large Spanish or yellow onions, halved and thinly sliced
2 cups water
1 quart vegetable stock (preferably onion-flavored)
1 bay leaf
1 teaspoon fresh thyme (or $1/2$ teaspoon dried)
$1/4$ cup sherry
$1/2$ teaspoon salt
$1/2$ teaspoon freshly ground black pepper
6 slices French bread, sliced about 1 inch thick and lightly toasted
6 tablespoons crumbled goat cheese or grated soy cheese, or to taste
Fresh thyme for garnish (optional)

Heat oil and margarine in a large skillet over medium-high heat. Add onions; sauté until tender and golden, 5 to 7 minutes. Transfer to a large saucepan with water and stock, and place over medium-high heat. Add bay leaf, thyme, sherry, salt and pepper; simmer 30 minutes.

Preheat oven to 500°F. Pour soup into 6 ovenproof serving bowls. Place a bread slice on top of each, and sprinkle about 1 tablespoon cheese over each bowl. Place bowls on a baking sheet; transfer to oven. Bake until cheese melts, 1 to 2 minutes. Garnish with thyme if desired, and serve.

Per Serving: 192 Calories; 5g Protein; 9g Fat; 23g Carbohydrates; 1mg Cholesterol; 917mg Sodium; 2g Fiber.

Potato-Pumpkin Soup

Use a firm, unblemished pie pumpkin.

8- to 10-pound pie pumpkin
2 medium boiling potatoes, peeled and chopped
2 medium white onions, chopped
6 cups water
1 teaspoon salt, or to taste
Freshly ground white pepper to taste
1 teaspoon dried thyme
1/2 cup condensed skimmed milk
2 tablespoons minced fresh parsley for garnish
Toasted pumpkin seeds for garnish (optional)

With a heavy knife, cut off top third of pumpkin. Scoop out seeds and strings; reserve seeds. Using a heavy spoon, scoop out pumpkin flesh, leaving a 1-inch wall inside. Refrigerate shell and top.

In a large, heavy kettle, combine potatoes, onions, 2 cups pumpkin flesh and water. Add salt, pepper and thyme. Bring to a boil, cover and cook over medium heat until vegetables are fork-tender, about 20 minutes.

Meanwhile, preheat oven to 200°F. Place pumpkin shell and top on a baking tray and place in oven to warm.

With a slotted spoon, remove vegetables from cooking water. Puree vegetables in a food processor fitted with a steel blade, or mash by hand until free of lumps. Return puree to cooking water. Stir in condensed milk, adding more if necessary to create a medium consistency. Heat gently over low heat for a few minutes, until hot. Do not allow to boil.

To serve, place pumpkin shell on a large serving tray. Pour in hot soup and sprinkle with parsley and toasted pumpkin seeds if desired. Cover with lid to keep warm.

HELPFUL HINT: *To toast pumpkin seeds, rinse seeds thoroughly and remove all strings and pulp. Allow to dry, then toss with 1 1/2 tablespoons oil and salt to taste. Bake at 350°F 20 to 30 minutes, stirring every 5 minutes, until seeds are golden brown.*

Per Serving: 188 Calories; 5g Protein; 3g Fat; 38g Carbohydrates; 9mg Cholesterol; 430mg Sodium; 4g Fiber.

Mushroom Wild Rice Chowder

This is practically a meal in itself.

Makes 6 servings

2 tablespoons vegetable oil
8 ounces fresh mushrooms, sliced
1 rib celery, thinly sliced
$^1/_2$ cup unbleached flour
$3^3/_4$ cups water
3 cups cooked wild rice
1 teaspoon salt
$^1/_2$ teaspoon curry powder
$^1/_2$ teaspoon dry mustard
$^1/_2$ teaspoon cinnamon
2 to 3 drops hot pepper sauce
$1^1/_2$ cups evaporated skimmed milk, half-and-half or soymilk
Paprika
$^1/_2$ cup toasted, slivered almonds (optional)

In a soup pot, heat oil. Add mushrooms and celery and sauté 2 minutes. Sprinkle flour over vegetables and cook over medium-low heat, stirring, 1 minute. Gradually add water, stirring constantly; cook over medium heat until mixture is somewhat thickened. Stir in remaining ingredients. Heat thoroughly. Garnish with paprika and toasted almonds if desired.

Per Serving: 224 Calories; 10g Protein; 5g Fat; 35g Carbohydrates; 2mg Cholesterol; 475mg Sodium; 2g Fiber.

Pumpkin Soup

Too many pumpkin soups rely on milk or cream for flavor and texture. This one depends upon vegetable broth, aromatic spices and fresh pumpkin puree for great flavor and texture. Fresh puree and homemade vegetable broth provide the best flavor. If you use canned pumpkin, boost the flavor by sautéing garlic, ginger and 1 teaspoon curry powder with the onion.

MAKES 8 SERVINGS
(8 CUPS)

1 tablespoon light olive oil
1 teaspoon ground cumin
1 teaspoon ground coriander
$\frac{1}{4}$ teaspoon cinnamon
2 cups diced yellow onion
2 cups fresh pumpkin puree or 15-ounce can pumpkin puree
6 cups vegetable stock
Salt to taste
$\frac{1}{4}$ cup thinly sliced scallion
$\frac{1}{2}$ cup toasted croutons

Heat oil in a 3½-quart saucepan. Add dry spices, stirring to warm but not browning, about 1 minute.

Add onion, stirring to coat. Sauté over medium heat until onion is soft but not brown, about 5 minutes. Add pumpkin puree and stock; stir to mix. Bring to a boil. Lower heat to a simmer. Simmer, covered, until soup is slightly thickened and flavors are melded, about 20 to 25 minutes. Salt to taste.

Pour soup into a large bowl. Puree in batches in a food processor or blender. Return to pan. Heat before serving. Garnish with scallions and croutons.

 Per Serving: 81 Calories; 2g Protein; 2g Fat; 15g Carbohydrates; 0mg Cholesterol; 353mg Sodium; 3g Fiber.

Mushroom Soup or Sauce

With a few simple variations, this soup goes vegan or becomes an all-purpose sauce.

MAKES 4 SERVINGS

1 tablespoon olive oil, canola oil or butter
1 pound mushrooms, thinly sliced or diced (see Note)
1 small onion, finely chopped
$\frac{1}{2}$ cup dry white wine
$2\frac{1}{2}$ cups vegetable stock or water (see Variation)
1 cup evaporated skimmed milk (see Variation)
1 teaspoon salt, or to taste
Freshly ground black pepper to taste

Heat oil or butter in a wide-bottomed saucepan over a medium flame. Add mushrooms and onion; sauté, stirring frequently, adding small amounts of wine to prevent sticking. Sauté until all wine is used and mushrooms are soft.

Add stock or water. Bring to a boil, reduce heat and simmer about 10 minutes. Add evaporated milk, salt and pepper; continue cooking until soup is heated through.

NOTE: *Shiitake, cremini or other exotic mushroom varieties make the most interesting soup, but white supermarket mushrooms are fine. Only the caps of shiitakes should be used, but the stems of most other mushrooms, unless they are dry and woody, can be incorporated.*

VARIATIONS:

- *If you omit the stock or water, this soup becomes an excellent multipurpose sauce. When you mix it with pasta or rice, add some chopped parsley, and perhaps some steamed broccoli or green beans.*

- *For a vegan soup, omit salt and substitute tomato juice for milk. To make a vegan sauce instead of a soup, add 1 cup of canned crushed tomatoes, omitting water. (Flavor this sauce with a little dried oregano, rosemary or thyme and 1 or 2 teaspoons garlic juice.) This is a combination you can pour over almost anything.*

Per Serving: 148 Calories; 9g Protein; 5g Fat; 16g Carbohydrates; 2mg Cholesterol; 1286mg Sodium; 2g Fiber.

Anasazi Bean Soup

The beans in this soup are one of the many heirloom seeds on the market today. You can recognize them by their red-and-white color.

MAKES 4 SERVINGS

1 cup dry Anasazi beans, picked over and rinsed
Vegetable stock or water
1 medium onion, chopped
2 large cloves garlic, pressed or minced
$\frac{1}{4}$ teaspoon ground coriander
$\frac{1}{2}$ teaspoon ground cumin
1 jalapeño or other pepper, finely chopped
Salt to taste
Minced green onions and/or cilantro leaves for garnish

Cover beans with water and soak overnight, allowing extra water for expansion. Drain, reserving soaking water. Measure soaking water and add stock or water to equal 6 cups. Pour into pot.

Add remaining ingredients except salt, green onion and/or cilantro and bring to a boil. Cover, reduce heat and cook at a low simmer 1½ to 2 hours, or until beans are tender. Season with salt to taste and serve hot, garnished with green onion and/or cilantro.

Per Serving: 168 Cal.; 11g Protein; 1g Fat; 31g Carbohydrates; 0mg Cholesterol; 72mg Sodium; 10g Fiber.

SALUBRIOUS
S a l a d s

*L*ike the introduction to a book or the opening minutes of a movie, the salad course greets the guests, so to speak, and commences the Thanksgiving dinner. A well-made salad is intended to cleanse and refresh the palate and set the stage for the meal to come. The salad course should be colorful, attractive and, from a cook's standpoint, easy to prepare and assemble. (On a jam-packed Thanksgiving Day, there is little time for fussing over the dinner salad!)

The bounty of seasonal salads in this chapter are guaranteed to jazz up any Thanksgiving menu. Recipes such as Warm Spinach Salad with Cranberry Dressing or Apple-Walnut Salad with Watercress are tangy autumn delights; other chilled dishes like the Asparagus Roll-Ups, Winter Pear Salad with Raspberry Vinaigrette and Aztec Platter give a creative gourmet twist to the holiday menu. These salads will please guests at any time of year but are especially enjoyed as starters to a Thanksgiving menu comprised of other dishes from this book.

It is a good idea to determine the main dish and side dishes prior to deciding on the salad entree. Ideally, the salad course should complement the main dish and side dishes and not include ingredients that appear in the later courses. If two substantial appetizers are to be served or a hearty soup is planned, a salad course may not be necessary. On the other hand, if appetizers or soups are not in the works, the opening salad course will be a welcome addition to the menu.

Greens with Tangerine-Ginger Vinaigrette

For best results, plan ahead and make the dressing with Orange Vinegar (see Note), which has to age for two weeks.

Makes 8 servings
(16 cups)

6 tablespoons fresh tangerine or orange juice
3 tablespoons Orange Vinegar (see Note) or sherry vinegar
1 teaspoon chopped fresh chives
$^1/_2$ teaspoon grated orange zest
$^1/_4$ teaspoon ground ginger
$^1/_4$ teaspoon ground anise or ground fennel seeds
Salt to taste
$^1/_2$ cup canola or olive oil
1 tangerine or orange, peeled and segmented
About 1 pound mesclun greens

To make the dressing, in a medium bowl, whisk together tangerine or orange juice, vinegar, chives, orange zest, ginger, anise or fennel and salt. Whisk in oil until well blended. Add tangerine or orange segments and toss to coat. Cover and chill for at least 1 hour, up to 24 hours.

To serve, put greens into large bowl. Add tangerine or orange sections and dressing, and toss to mix and coat.

Per Serving: 78 Calories; 1g Protein; 7g Fat; 4g Carbohydrates; 0mg Cholesterol; 6mg Sodium; 1g Fiber.

NOTE: *To make Orange Vinegar, put several orange or tangerine peels, about 2 tablespoons chopped fresh chives and ¼ teaspoon minced fresh ginger root into a 1-pint jar. Fill jar with apple cider vinegar, then cap and age for two weeks. Store vinegar in a cool, dry place away from light.*

Warm Spinach Salad with Cranberry Dressing

This unique dressing makes a tossed salad something special.

MAKES 8 SERVINGS

RELISH
12-ounce bag cranberries
1 orange, quartered, including peel
2 to 3 tablespoons honey or sugar, or to taste

DRESSING
1 cup cranberry relish
1 to 2 tablespoons honey or sugar, or to taste
1 teaspoon salt
1 teaspoon freshly ground black pepper
1 tablespoon freshly grated ginger root
Pinch freshly grated nutmeg
2 cups walnut oil or olive oil

SALAD
2 pounds fresh spinach, stemmed
Walnut halves, mandarin orange sections and cranberry relish for garnish

To make the relish, place all ingredients in a food processor. Pulse until finely chopped, about 20 seconds. Transfer 1 cup cranberry relish to food processor. Reserve remaining relish.

To make the dressing, place all ingredients except oil in food processor with cranberry relish; pulse a few times to blend. With machine running, slowly add oil until incorporated. Transfer to a saucepan. Heat over low heat until warmed through.

To make the salad, in a large salad bowl, toss together spinach and salad dressing to taste. Garnish with walnuts, orange sections and reserved cranberry relish.

VARIATION: *Serve the cranberry relish on its own with salad, or as a side dish.*

HELPFUL HINT: *You can reduce preparation time by using frozen, prepared cranberry relish.*

Per Serving (with 2 Tablespoons Dressing): 203 Calories; 3g Protein; 18g Fat; 9g Carbohydrates; 0mg Cholesterol; 187mg Sodium; 4g Fiber.

Aztec Platter

This composed salad is beautiful enough to impress company, but it's also simple enough to prepare for an everyday meal. It's fast—only 30 minutes to the table.

MAKES 6 SERVINGS

QUINOA-CORN SALAD
1 cup quinoa, well rinsed
$\frac{1}{2}$ cup cooked fresh or frozen corn kernels
Juice of 1 lemon (about 3 tablespoons)
2 to 3 scallions, minced
1 tablespoon olive oil
Salt and freshly ground black pepper to taste

BEAN SALAD
$1\frac{1}{2}$ cups cooked or canned pinto, kidney or Anasazi beans
1 heaping cup finely diced ripe tomatoes
1 tablespoon balsamic or cider vinegar
$\frac{1}{4}$ cup chopped fresh parsley
Salt and freshly ground black pepper to taste (salt not necessary
    if using canned beans)

GARNISH
Pumpkin seeds
Black olives
Red pepper or pimientos, cut into narrow strips about $1\frac{1}{2}$ inches long

To make the quinoa-corn salad, bring 2 cups water to a boil in a small, heavy saucepan. Add quinoa and simmer gently, covered, for 15 minutes. Fluff with a fork, then let cool to room temperature. Transfer to a mixing bowl and combine with remaining ingredients.

To make the bean salad, in a separate bowl, combine all ingredients and toss together.

To assemble, transfer quinoa-corn salad onto center of platter. Make a well in center about 5 inches in diameter. Mound bean salad in well. Sprinkle with pumpkin seeds. Arrange olives and strips of pepper or pimientos around rim of platter.

Per Serving: 198 Calories; 7g Protein; 4g Fat; 35g Carbohydrates; 0mg Cholesterol; 300mg Sodium; 5g Fiber.

Asparagus Roll-Ups

Use soft lettuces such as butter or red oak for this appetizer or salad.

1 cup low-fat mayonnaise
1 tablespoon chopped sun-dried tomatoes
3 scallions, finely chopped (white and green parts)
16 lettuce leaves, washed and dried
32 large asparagus spears, lightly cooked and drained
16 sprigs fresh dill weed
Edible flowers for garnish (optional)
Steamed scallion strips (optional)

In a small bowl, mix mayonnaise, sun-dried tomatoes and chopped scallions. With a teaspoon, spread a little mixture inside each lettuce leaf. Top with 2 asparagus spears. Add 1 sprig dill weed and 1 edible flower if desired.

Roll to form a "bouquet"; tie with scallion strips. Place on a serving platter. Repeat until all ingredients are used. Chill until ready to serve.

Per Serving: 56 Calories; 1g Protein; 5g Fat; 2g Carbohydrates; 0mg Cholesterol; 117mg Sodium; 1g Fiber.

Black-Eyed Pea, Corn and Sweet Potato Salad

Here is a colorful, tasty sweet-sour salad.

MAKES 6 SERVINGS

2 cups diced sweet potatoes, unpeeled
2 tablespoons vegetable oil
2 tablespoons red wine vinegar
3 tablespoons minced fresh parsley ($1^1/_2$ tablespoons dried)
1 teaspoon Dijon mustard
$^1/_2$ teaspoon freshly ground black pepper
$^1/_4$ teaspoon salt
Two 16-ounce cans black-eyed peas, drained
$1^1/_2$ cups fresh or thawed frozen corn kernels
2 green onions, finely chopped

Cook sweet potato in boiling water to cover until tender, about 15 minutes. Drain and rinse under cold running water.

Meanwhile, in a large mixing bowl, whisk together oil, vinegar, parsley, mustard, pepper and salt. Stir in black-eyed peas, corn, green onions and sweet potatoes. Chill for 1 hour before serving.

Per Serving: 207 Calories; 8g Protein; 5g Fat; 38g Carbohydrates; 0mg Cholesterol; 662mg Sodium; 5g Fiber.

Winter Pear Salad in Raspberry Vinaigrette

This crunchy salad contains a wonderful mélange of flavors. Serve it on individual salad plates at each place setting, or arrange it on a large, round tray at the buffet table.

MAKES 15 SERVINGS

SALAD
8 cups torn radicchio
10 Bosc pears, cored and thinly sliced
1 cup gorgonzola, crumbled feta or shaved Parmesan cheese
2 cups chopped toasted walnuts
$1/2$ cup chopped fresh Italian parsley
1 cup fresh raspberries (optional)

VINAIGRETTE
$1/2$ cup raspberry vinegar
$1/2$ cup extra-virgin olive oil
1 teaspoon salt
1 teaspoon freshly ground black pepper

To make the salad, arrange an attractive bed of torn radicchio leaves on salad plates or a large platter. Arrange pear slices on radicchio in fan shapes. Thinly slice or crumble cheese over pears. Sprinkle walnuts, parsley and raspberries, if desired, over salad.

To make the vinaigrette, place all ingredients in a jar and shake to combine. Just before serving, drizzle vinaigrette over salad.

Per Serving: 272 Calories; 7g Protein; 21g Fat; 18g Carbohydrates; 15mg Cholesterol; 349mg Sodium; 3g Fiber.

Simple-but-Symbolic Apple Salad

This beautiful and tempting salad of red apple and crisp greens is dressed with lemon vinaigrette.

MAKES 2 SERVINGS

2 handfuls fresh salad greens (such as spinach, romaine, Boston
   or leaf lettuce; avoid iceberg and bitter greens)
2 teaspoons olive oil
1 red apple, cored and diced
Splash of fresh lemon juice
Salt and freshly ground black pepper to taste
Lemon slices for garnish

Tear greens into bite-sized pieces; toss in a large bowl with oil. Set aside. Sprinkle apple with lemon juice, salt and pepper.

To serve, arrange a bed of greens on 2 plates; sprinkle with apple. Garnish with lemon.

Per Serving: 84 Calories; 1g Protein; 5g Fat; 11g Carbohydrates; 0mg Cholesterol; 271mg Sodium; 3g Fiber.

Roasted Asparagus Salad

Fresh orange and lime juices give this light salad plenty of flavor.

Makes 6 servings

1 pound asparagus, trimmed and cut diagonally into $\frac{1}{2}$-inch pieces
    (about $2\frac{2}{3}$ cups)
Olive oil spray
Herbal salt to taste
$\frac{1}{2}$ cup fresh orange juice
1 tablespoon fresh lime juice
2 tablespoons orange marmalade
$\frac{1}{2}$ teaspoon freshly grated ginger root
1 to 2 tablespoons olive oil
7 cups chopped romaine lettuce
3 tablespoons pine nuts or slivered almonds, toasted

Preheat oven to 450°F. Spread asparagus on a baking sheet in a single layer; mist lightly with olive oil spray. Roast until asparagus is tender when pierced with a knife, about 10 to 12 minutes. Season with herbal salt; set aside.

In a blender or bowl, mix juices, marmalade, ginger root and olive oil; process until well blended. Before serving, arrange lettuce on individual plates or on a platter; top with asparagus. Whisk dressing again; pour over salad. Garnish with pine nuts or almonds.

Per Serving: 64 Calories; 2g Protein; 4g Fat; 6g Carbohydrates; 0mg Cholesterol; 27mg Sodium; 2g Fiber.

Corn, Sweet Potato and Green Bean Salad

This tricolored salad is even tastier with a sprinkling of balsamic vinegar.

MAKES 4 SERVINGS

1 pound sweet potatoes, peeled and cut into 1-inch cubes
2 cups 1$\frac{1}{2}$-inch-long green beans
1 cup thawed frozen corn
$\frac{1}{4}$ to $\frac{1}{2}$ cup Balsamic Dressing (recipe follows)
Salt to taste
Balsamic vinegar for sprinkling (optional)
4 hard-boiled eggs, quartered (optional)
Roasted pumpkin seeds or sunflower seeds for garnish

Steam sweet potatoes 15 to 18 minutes, or until tender. Steam green beans 6 to 8 minutes, or until tender. Steam corn 3 to 4 minutes. Place all vegetables in a large bowl; stir in dressing. Add salt.

Sprinkle with balsamic vinegar if desired. Arrange eggs on top if desired; scatter with seeds.

Per Serving (with 1 Tablespoon Dressing): 240 Calories; 5g Protein; 11g Fat; 36g Carbohydrates; 0mg Cholesterol; 143mg Sodium; 3g Fiber.

Balsamic Dressing

Use this dressing on the Corn, Sweet Potato and Green Bean Salad. And when you're done, save any extra to use on salads throughout the week.

Makes ½ cup
(8 tablespoons)

6 tablespoons olive oil
2 tablespoons balsamic vinegar
1 teaspoon minced garlic
½ teaspoon sugar
¼ teaspoon salt

Place all ingredients in a lidded jar. Close jar; shake thoroughly. Chill until ready to serve. Shake again before using.

HELPFUL HINT: *Dressing is best if made at least 30 minutes ahead of time.*

Per Tablespoon: 92 Calories; 1g Protein; 10g Fat; 1g Carbohydrate; 0mg Cholesterol, 133mg Sodium; 0mg Fiber.

Corn-Olive Salad

Here's a colorful and oh-so-easy salad. It's a cinch to make ahead of time during the busy Thanksgiving preparations.

Makes 6 servings

16-ounce package frozen corn kernels, thawed
1 medium red or green bell pepper, cut into 1-inch strips
$\frac{1}{4}$ cup black olives, coarsely chopped
$\frac{1}{4}$ cup green olives, coarsely chopped
1 celery stalk, diced
1 scallion, finely chopped
1 tablespoon olive oil
3 tablespoons apple cider vinegar
1 teaspoon honey
$\frac{1}{2}$ teaspoon dried dill
Freshly ground black pepper to taste

Combine all ingredients in a large bowl and mix thoroughly. Place in refrigerator until ready to serve.

*Per Serving: 98 Calories; 2g Protein; 5g Fat; 13g Carbohydrates; 0mg Cholesterol; 240mg Sodium; 1g Fiber.

Toasted Corn Salad with Citrus Vinaigrette

Think there's nothing you can do with leftovers when you aren't serving turkey? Serve this salad with toasted slices of Corn Batter Bread (see recipe, page 000) for a simple lunch or supper.

MAKES 11 SERVINGS.

SALAD
1 cup fresh corn kernels
2 quarts (about 8 cups or 10-ounce bag) mixed baby salad greens
¾ cup cooked black beans
½ cup cooked rice
1 cup seeded, finely chopped cherry tomatoes

VINAIGRETTE
1 clove garlic, minced
¼ cup freshly squeezed lime juice (2 limes)
½ cup freshly squeezed lemon juice (3 lemons)
½ cup freshly squeezed orange juice (1 medium orange)
½ teaspoon orange zest
1 tablespoon rice or other mild white vinegar
2 teaspoons Dijon mustard
1 teaspoon salt
1 teaspoon honey
¼ cup corn oil
½ cup canola oil

In a large, hot, nonstick dry skillet over high heat, toast corn kernels until they "jump" and char slightly, flipping often with a spatula. When kernels are toasted, turn out on paper towels to cool.

To a blender jar, food processor bowl or jar with lid, add garlic, citrus juices, zest, vinegar, mustard, salt and honey. Process or shake to mix thoroughly. With motor running or while whisking, add oils in a thin stream. Set aside.

In a large salad bowl, add greens, beans, rice, tomatoes and corn. Toss with a small amount of vinaigrette, starting with ¼ cup. Add more by tablespoon to taste.

VARIATION: *Add 4 to 6 pickled jalapeño slices to blender or food processor, or mince and add to jar.*

HELPFUL HINT: *To get the most juice out of limes, use your palms to roll them back and forth firmly across countertop to soften. Then cut and juice with a citrus juicer or reamer.*

🌿 Per Serving (1 Cup Salad with 1 Tablespoon Vinaigrette): 141 Calories; 3g Protein; 6g Fat; 20g Carbohydrates; 0mg Cholesterol; 90mg Sodium; 2g Fiber.

Apple-Walnut Salad with Watercress

This salad is colorful and refreshing.

MAKES 5 SERVINGS

DRESSING
2 tablespoons fresh lemon juice
2 tablespoons vegetable broth
$1\frac{1}{2}$ tablespoons vegetable oil
$\frac{1}{2}$ teaspoon salt (or 1 teaspoon soy sauce)
$\frac{1}{4}$ teaspoon freshly ground black pepper

SALAD
2 cups watercress, tough stems removed
1 large carrot, shredded
1 red Delicious apple, cored and shredded
1 golden Delicious apple, cored and shredded
2 tablespoons fresh lemon juice
$\frac{1}{4}$ to $\frac{1}{2}$ cup chopped walnuts

To make the dressing, in a small bowl, combine all dressing ingredients. Mix well.

To prepare the salad, place watercress around the outside edge of a large platter. Scatter carrot next to the watercress. In a small bowl, toss shredded apples with lemon juice. Spoon apples into center of platter. Scatter nuts on top of apples. Pour dressing over the salad and serve immediately.

🌿 Per Serving (1 Cup Salad with 1 Tablespoon Dressing): 121 Calories; 2g Protein; 8g Fat; 13g Carbohydrates; 0mg Cholesterol; 271mg Sodium; 3g Fiber.

MAGNIFICENT
Entrees

Ever since the Pilgrims and Native Ameri-
ans first sat down together in 1620, it seems that turkey has been inextricably
linked with Thanksgiving. The obvious repercussion, of course, is that hosting the
big holiday dinner without serving a turkey front-and-center has been a daunting
proposition for most vegetarians. The annual quandary has always been what to
serve in place of the turkey. This chapter answers that query with an enticing list
of meatless dishes perfect for the autumn celebration. The message is clear:
Dispense with the turkey, and a world of culinary possibilities opens up.

Here, finally, is a vast array of vegetarian main dishes that will grace the
Thanksgiving table with style and fabulous flavor. From Baked Pumpkin with
Vegetable Pilaf and Autumn Risotto with Squash and Spinach to Mushroom-
Pecan Stew and Herb and Walnut Ravioli, a variety of splendid main courses will
rejuvenate and enliven the traditional Thanksgiving dinner. Your harvest table will
beckon with dishes inspired by autumn vegetables, pumpkins, root vegetables
and winter squash galore. Recipes fortified with whole grains, rice and beans

offer hearty sustenance, while a plethora of herbs and spices contribute delectable nuances. Ordinary ingredients are transformed into extraordinary dishes.

Since the main dish is the star attraction of the Thanksgiving menu, the best advice is to decide what it will be at an early stage in the meal planning. Also, keep in mind that the main dish should be artfully displayed, easy to serve and, most of all, a pleasure to devour. (If you are going to spend extra time in the kitchen, spend it on the entree.) Once you have settled on the main dish, choose a medley of side dishes and sauces to bring complementary flavors and colors to the table.

Turkey or no turkey, every Thanksgiving deserves an impressive centerpiece to symbolize the festive sentiments and fanfare of the season—and this chapter will help you create one. Before you know it, the notion of seeing a turkey on Thanksgiving will fade to a distant memory. Some traditions, like rules, were meant to be broken.

Layered Seitan Vegetable Dinner

The hearty flavor and texture of seitan makes it a perfect choice for a Thanksgiving meal. By layering the vegetables in the pot, they will retain their shape and individual flavors.

MAKES 4 SERVINGS

1 large onion, diced in ³/₄-inch pieces
1 tablespoon extra-virgin olive oil
4 cloves garlic, chopped
1 teaspoon dried basil
¹/₂ teaspoon dried thyme
¹/₂ teaspoon dried oregano
¹/₂ teaspoon ground coriander seed
¹/₄ teaspoon ground cumin seed
1 dried bay leaf
8-ounce package seitan, drained and cut into 1-inch chunks
Freshly ground black pepper to taste
2 medium carrots, peeled and cut into ³/₄-inch chunks
2 ribs celery, cut into 1-inch pieces
1 pound boiling potatoes, cut into ³/₄-inch chunks
¹/₂ pound mushrooms, chopped
1¹/₂ cups vegetable stock or water
1 small butternut squash, peeled, seeded and cut into ³/₄-inch chunks
1 tablespoon fresh lemon juice
1 small bunch kale, chopped
Sea salt to taste

In a heavy-bottomed 3-quart stew pot, sauté onion in oil until soft, 3 to 4 minutes. Add garlic, herbs and spices and continue to cook for 1 minute longer, stirring to incorporate the seasonings.

Place seitan on top of onions and season with pepper. Continue to layer with carrots, celery, potatoes and mushrooms. Do not stir.

Add stock or water to just cover layer of mushrooms. Simmer, covered, for 15 minutes. Add squash on top of mushrooms, cover and cook 15 minutes longer, until squash is just tender. Add lemon juice.

Remove the lid, add kale and cook 5 minutes longer. Remove bay leaf. Check seasonings and add salt and additional pepper as needed. Serve hot.

Per Serving: 300 Calories; 22g Protein; 5g Fat; 48g Carbohydrates; 0mg Cholesterol; 547mg Sodium; 7g Fiber.

Vegetable Pancakes with Roasted Plum Sauce

These entree pancakes are delicious on their own, but with the addition of fresh plum sauce, they are unforgettable. The pancakes can be made up ahead of time and rewarmed, helping to make your day less hectic.

Makes 4 pancakes
(4 servings)

SAUCE
4 plums, pitted and quartered, or equivalent frozen peach slices
1 tablespoon grated fresh ginger root
1 tablespoon fresh lemon juice
$\frac{1}{2}$ tablespoon tamari or soy sauce
Pinch cayenne

PANCAKES
1 medium boiling potato, peeled
1 zucchini
1 yellow squash
1 small Spanish onion, peeled
$\frac{1}{2}$ teaspoon salt
$\frac{1}{2}$ teaspoon freshly ground black pepper
1 garlic clove, finely minced
$\frac{1}{4}$ cup chopped chives
2 tablespoons olive oil, divided in half

To make the sauce, preheat oven to 400°F. Combine all ingredients in a mixing bowl; toss to mix. Let sit for 15 minutes to extract fruit juices. Transfer fruit to baking dish; bake until fruit is dark and juices are thick, about 15 minutes, stirring occasionally. Remove from oven. Puree in blender until smooth. Set aside until ready to serve; serve at room temperature.

To make the pancakes, grate potato into mixing bowl. Grate zucchini, squash and onion into same bowl. Add salt, pepper, garlic and chives, and toss to combine. Let stand for 20 minutes.

Heat 1 tablespoon of the oil in a large nonstick sauté pan over medium heat. Squeeze potato mixture in a clean, dry tea towel to extract moisture. Divide mixture into 4 portions; sprinkle 2 portions evenly over bottom of pan, spreading with 2 forks to form 2 thin pancakes. Cook until golden, about 5 minutes. Flip and cook other side until golden brown, about 3 minutes. Repeat with remaining mixture, adding more oil if needed. Drain pancakes well on paper towels after cooking.

🍂 Per Serving (with 1 Tablespoon Sauce): 155 Calories; 2g Protein; 7g Fat; 21g Carbohydrates; 0mg Cholesterol; 298mg Sodium; 3g Fiber.

Green Rice with Winter Squash

For Thanksgiving, serve the rice in baked acorn squash halves.

Makes 6 servings

1 tablespoon canola oil
1 medium onion, chopped (1 cup)
3 or 4 cloves garlic, minced
1 large jalapeño pepper, seeded and minced
3 cups chopped fresh spinach or kale
$3\frac{1}{2}$ cups water
2 cups diced winter squash
$1\frac{1}{2}$ cups uncooked long-grain white or brown rice
$1\frac{1}{2}$ teaspoons ground cumin
1 teaspoon salt
$\frac{1}{2}$ teaspoon freshly ground black pepper
$\frac{1}{4}$ cup chopped fresh parsley
4 green onions (white and pale green parts), chopped

In a medium saucepan, heat oil over medium heat. Add onion, garlic and jalapeño, and cook, stirring often, until vegetables begin to soften, about 5 minutes. Add spinach or kale and cook, stirring often, until wilted, about 3 minutes. Add water, squash, rice and dry seasonings and bring to a boil. Reduce heat; cover and simmer until rice and squash are tender and liquid is absorbed, about 20 minutes (if using brown rice, about 30 minutes). Fluff rice with fork and stir in parsley and green onions.

Per Serving: 154 Calories; 4g Protein; 3g Fat; 29g Carbohydrates; 0mg Cholesterol; 459mg Sodium; 2g Fiber.

Pattypan Squash Stuffed with Split Peas

Scalloped pattypan squash make a stunning container for yellow split peas. You can use medium-sized squash for a main or side dish, or if the baby variety is available, serve as a first course or as hors d'oeuvres.

MAKES 8 SERVINGS

3 tablespoons peanut or vegetable oil
3 small shallots, finely chopped
2 jalapeño peppers, seeded and chopped
$^1/_3$ cup chopped fresh dill
$^1/_3$ cup dried yellow split peas, rinsed and drained
1 cup water, plus 1 tablespoon
$^3/_4$ teaspoon salt
8 medium or 24 baby pattypan squash

In a medium saucepan, heat oil over medium heat. Add shallots and cook, stirring often, until soft, about 2 minutes. Add jalapeños and dill and cook, stirring often, 2 minutes. Add split peas, 1 cup water and salt. Bring to a boil. Reduce heat to low, cover and simmer until peas are tender but still hold their shape, 25 to 30 minutes. Let stand covered for 5 minutes. If liquid is not absorbed, drain mixture.

Cut squash in half crosswise. In a large nonstick skillet, brown squash over medium heat. Add 1 tablespoon water, and cover and cook until tender, 10 to 12 minutes. Spoon split-pea mixture into squash halves.

Per Serving: 77 Calories; 2g Protein; 7g Fat; 5g Carbohydrates; 0mg Cholesterol; 259mg Sodium; 1g Fiber.

Golden Lentil Roulade with Chestnut Stuffing

This roulade is different from most in that its outer layer, which is made of cooked lentils, is unbaked when it is rolled around the stuffing; baking is done after rolling. This allows the dish to be assembled well in advance. Want Thanksgiving leftovers? These can be eaten cold—the roulade slices like a dream and is great on a sandwich with pickles or alongside a salad.

MAKES 8 SERVINGS

1½ cups red lentils
2½ cups water
3 cloves garlic, chopped
3 tablespoons water or fresh lemon juice
2 cups fresh bread crumbs
½ teaspoon salt
¼ teaspoon freshly ground black pepper
2 tablespoons soft butter or margarine

STUFFING
1 tablespoon vegetable oil
2 medium onions, peeled and chopped (2 cups)
1 cup finely chopped red bell pepper
1½ cups canned peeled chestnuts
2 cups fresh bread crumbs
¼ cup chopped fresh sage
Salt and freshly ground black pepper to taste
½ cup chopped fresh parsley
Sprigs fresh sage for garnish

In a medium saucepan, combine lentils and 2½ cups water. Bring to a boil. Reduce heat, cover and simmer until lentils are tender and water is absorbed, about 15 minutes.

To make the stuffing, in a medium skillet, heat oil over medium heat. Add onions and bell pepper and cook, stirring often, until vegetables are soft, about 7 minutes. Remove from heat. In a food processor, combine onion-pepper mixture, chestnuts, bread crumbs and chopped sage; pulse on and off until well blended. Transfer to a large bowl and season with salt and pepper.

Preheat oven to 350°F. Transfer cooked lentils to a food processor. Add garlic, water or lemon juice, bread crumbs, salt and pepper, and process until mixture becomes a smooth, pliable dough. Spread out a large piece parchment paper or wax paper on a flat surface. Transfer lentil mixture to paper and pat into an 11-by-14-inch rectangle. Spread chestnut mixture evenly over lentil layer. Starting with a short end, carefully roll up lentil mixture, using paper to guide you (pull upward on edge of paper to propel the dough forward and create a rolling action). Press roll firmly together with your hands as needed. Lift roulade onto a lightly greased baking sheet; rub softened butter or margarine over it. Bake until heated through and top is just beginning to brown, 15 to 20 minutes. Transfer to a serving platter. Garnish with sprigs of sage.

Per Serving: 359 Calories; 16g Protein; 7g Fat; 58g Carbohydrates; 8mg Cholesterol; 475mg Sodium; 14g Fiber.

Acorn Squash Tortellini

Tortellini are circles of pasta that are filled and formed into rings. Legend has it that this pasta shape was inspired by Venus' belly button. Acorn squash lends this dish a distinctly American flavor—just right for Thanksgiving!

MAKES 6 SERVINGS

1 acorn squash
$^{1}/_{4}$ teaspoon ground nutmeg
$^{1}/_{4}$ teaspoon ground cinnamon
$^{1}/_{4}$ teaspoon honey
1 recipe Fresh Pasta Dough (page 77)

Preheat oven to 400°F. Slice squash in half lengthwise. Remove seeds and strings and place squash halves, cut side down, on a lightly oiled baking dish. Bake 45 minutes, until tender. Remove squash from oven and allow to cool. Scoop out flesh into a bowl and discard shell. With a fork, mash squash with nutmeg, cinnamon and honey. With a pasta machine or rolling pin, roll out a sheet of pasta dough. Use a cookie cutter or juice glass to cut dough into circles about 2½ inches in diameter. Place ½ teaspoon of filling about ½ inch from the edge of each circle. Fold each circle in half and press edges together. Pick up circle with your index finger and thumb, holding folded edge up. Pull up corners together around your index finger. Press corners together to seal, then flip up rim. Remove to a floured plate. Repeat with remaining dough and filling.

Boil pasta in a large pot of salted water for 2 minutes. Drain and add sauce of your choice.

Per Serving: 310 Calories; 11g Protein; 5g Fat; 60g Carbohydrates; 110mg Cholesterol; 41mg Sodium; 2g Fiber.

Carrot and Leek Tortellacci

Tortellacci means "big, bad tortellini." These larger pasta packets hold twice as much filling as tortellini.

MAKES 6 SERVINGS

10 small carrots
4 leeks
1 shallot
2 teaspoons extra-virgin olive oil
1 recipe Fresh Pasta Dough (page 77)
½ teaspoon salt

Peel carrots, and clean and trim leeks. Chop both into matchsticks 1 inch long and ¼ inch wide. Mince shallot. Sauté carrots, leeks and shallot in oil over low heat for 2 minutes. Add enough water to cover and braise over medium heat until vegetables are tender, about 15 minutes. Stir occasionally and add water as needed to keep skillet from boiling dry. Drain in a colander and let cool to room temperature.

With a pasta machine or rolling pin, roll out a sheet of pasta dough. Use a cookie cutter or juice glass to cut dough into circles about 2½ inches in diameter. Place a teaspoon of filling in the center of half of the pasta circle. Top each with a second circle and seal edges. Remove to a floured plate. Repeat with remaining dough and filling.

Boil pasta in a large pot of salted water for 2 minutes or until done. Drain and add sauce of your choice.

Per Serving: 364 Calories; 12g Protein; 6g Fat; 67g Carbohydrates; 110mg Cholesterol; 288mg Sodium; 7g Fiber.

Herb and Walnut Ravioli

The filling in these ravioli is like a mild, inexpensive pesto.

MAKES 6 SERVINGS

1 cup walnuts
3 cups lightly packed fresh basil
3 cups lightly packed fresh Italian parsley
¼ teaspoon salt, or to taste
1 recipe Fresh Pasta Dough (page 77)

Toast walnuts in a 350°F oven for 8 minutes. Meanwhile, rinse basil and parsley and pat dry. Discard stems and chop herbs very finely until they almost form a paste. (This step can be done with a mortar and pestle or food processor.) Chop nuts by hand into small crumbs and mix with herbs. Season with salt.

With a pasta machine or rolling pin, roll an egg-sized ball of pasta dough into a rectangle or circle and cut into strips about 2 inches wide and 12 inches long. Place one strip on a floured surface and dot it with teaspoonfuls of filling about 1 inch apart from each other. Place a second strip of pasta on top. Press down around the portions of filling, then cut into squares with a knife or pastry crimper. Press edges together a second time to be sure they stick, then remove to a floured plate. Repeat with remaining dough and filling.

Boil pasta in a large pot of salted water for 2 minutes or until done. Drain and add sauce of your choice.

Per Serving: 393 Calories; 14g Protein; 17g Fat; 50g Carbohydrates; 110mg Cholesterol; 153mg Sodium; 4g Fiber.

Fresh Pasta Dough

Making pasta dough may seem complicated, but with a little practice it's really easy.

MAKES 6 SERVINGS

About 3 cups unbleached white flour (see Notes)
4 eggs (or 1 cup egg substitute or 1 cup hot water—see Notes)

To make pasta by hand, pour flour onto a flat surface, forming a mound. Make a well (a deep indentation) in the center. Crack eggs into well and break up yolks with a fork. (Or pour in the egg substitute or hot water.) With your fingers, begin drawing in a little bit of flour at a time and mixing it with eggs or water. When mixture forms a paste, draw in all the flour. Mix well and begin kneading. Knead about 8 minutes, until you have a soft, firm ball of dough. Wrap in a damp dish towel.

If using a food processor, insert metal blades in the processor, pour 1½ cups flour and crack 2 eggs on top. (Or start processor and pour in half the egg substitute or hot water through the tube.) Process until dough forms a ball on top of the blades and cleans the sides of the bowl, about 1 minute. Then process 2 more minutes to knead it. Remove dough and wrap in a damp dish towel. Repeat process with remaining flour and eggs (or egg substitute and hot water).

To shape pasta, remove a piece of dough appropriate for the recipe you are making (an egg-sized piece for ravioli, a larger piece for tortellini and tortellacci). Keep remaining dough covered with dish towel. Roll out dough with a pasta machine or rolling pin until it is almost translucent. (Use the thinnest setting on your machine.) Cut into shapes needed for the dish you are making and add filling if necessary. Try to use up as much of the rolled-out pasta as possible the first time. (You can collect the trimmings and roll them again, but rolling too many times toughens the dough.) Repeat with remaining dough.

To cook, bring a large pot of water to a rolling boil and add a pinch of salt. Add fresh pasta and stir gently. It will begin bobbing to the surface after 1 to 2 minutes, indicating that it's almost ready. Stir and cook another 30 seconds or until it tastes done. Pasta should be served al dente, or slightly firm. Do not let fresh pasta overcook, or it will stick together and become sloppy.

NOTES:

- *The amount of flour you will need can vary greatly, depending on the size of your eggs, the batch your flour comes from and even the weather. If the dough is wet or is sticking to your hands rather than forming a soft ball, add 1 teaspoon of flour at a time, kneading between additions, until the dough reaches the right consistency. If the dough is dry and crumbly, add 1 teaspoon of water at a time, kneading between additions, until it reaches the right consistency.*

- *If you use water instead of eggs or egg substitute, the water should be hot from the tap, not boiling. This version is somewhat stickier than the egg or egg substitute methods, so be extra careful about flouring the rolling pin, work surface and your hands.*

🌿 Per Serving: 248 Calories; 10g Protein; 4g Fat; 43g Carbohydrates; 110mg Cholesterol; 36mg Sodium; 2g Fiber.

Mushroom Bourguignonne in a Whole Pumpkin

This entree looks festive on the holiday table.

MAKES 6 SERVINGS

5 to 6 pound kabocha squash or sugar pie pumpkin
2 large yellow or red onions, chopped
1 to 2 tablespoons water
1 pound mushrooms, halved (about 5 to 6 cups)
4 tablespoons unbleached white flour or whole-wheat pastry flour
2 to 2½ cups dry red wine
¼ cup soy sauce
2 to 3 cubes vegetable bouillon (optional)
½ teaspoon dried rosemary
3 tablespoons dry sherry or cooking sherry
1 tablespoon honey
2 tablespoons balsamic vinegar
Freshly ground black pepper
4 cloves garlic

With a very sharp, small knife, carve a 3- to 4-inch zig-zagged circle in the top of the squash or pumpkin and remove top. (If peel is too thick to cut easily, bake at 350°F 15 to 20 minutes to soften it.) Remove and discard seeds, and use a large spoon to scrape out the strings until the inside surface is clean.

In a heavy skillet, sauté onions in water for a few minutes. Add mushrooms; cover and simmer for a few minutes, until they have begun to excrete their juices. Stir in flour and cook 1 minute. Then add 2 cups red wine and remaining ingredients; cook about 15 minutes, stirring frequently. Pour stew into the squash, place in a large, shallow dish (such as a pie plate) and put the top of the squash back on. Bake at 350°F about 1 hour, or until squash is very soft. While baking, stir the stew a couple of times, adding ½ cup wine if too much liquid evaporates or is absorbed. To serve, spoon out some stew and scrape out some of the squash onto each plate.

🍂 Per Serving: 269 Calories; 8g Protein; 1g Fat; 49g Carbohydrates; 0mg Cholesterol; 710mg Sodium; 7g Fiber.

Carol's Seitan Roast with Mushroom Gravy

This delicious seitan recipe has been successful at celebratory dinners with vegetarians and non-vegetarians alike.

MAKES 6 SERVINGS

1 pound seitan
2 cups mushrooms
2 cups sliced onions
1.3-ounce package of Fantastic Foods Tofu Scrambler (half a 2.7-ounce box)
4 cups water
1 tablespoon chopped fresh basil leaves (or 1 teaspoon dry basil)
1 tablespoon chopped fresh sage leaves (or 1 teaspoon ground sage)

Slice seitan into ½-inch slices and place in a Dutch oven. Layer mushrooms and onions on top. In a bowl, combine dry Tofu Scrambler with water, basil and sage. Pour over seitan and vegetables. Bring to a boil over medium-high heat, then reduce heat to medium, cover pot and simmer 30 minutes, or until gravy has thickened and vegetables are soft. Serve hot.

🍂 Per Serving: 118 Calories; 22g Protein; 0g Fat; 8g Carbohydrates; 0mg Cholesterol; 299mg Sodium; 2g Fiber.

Spinach Roulade

Here is an exceptionally beautiful dish. A flat soufflé rolled around a spinach filling makes a pretty green-and-yellow spiral when sliced. The slices are set in a red-orange roasted pepper sauce and garnished with basil leaves.

MAKES 6 SERVINGS

SOUFFLÉ
Baker's parchment paper
Butter or oil for greasing pan
Butter or oil for treating paper
4 tablespoons butter
$^1/_3$ cup all-purpose flour
$1^3/_4$ cups milk, warmed
$^1/_2$ teaspoon salt
Freshly ground pepper
Dash freshly grated nutmeg
5 eggs, separated
$^1/_2$ cup freshly grated Parmesan cheese
Milk or light cream to brush on roulade before baking

FILLING
3 large bunches spinach (about $2^1/_2$ pounds)
1 onion, minced
2 tablespoons chopped fresh marjoram leaves (or 1 teaspoon dried marjoram)
1 tablespoon olive oil
Salt and freshly ground black pepper to taste
1 cup grated Gruyère cheese

GARNISH
Red Pepper Sauce (recipe follows)
Fresh basil leaves

To prepare the soufflé, cut a piece of parchment paper about an inch larger than a 10-by-15-inch jelly-roll pan. Lightly butter or oil pan, then press paper against it, making creases in the corners so that it will fit well. Lightly butter or oil paper, then sprinkle with flour. Set aside.

Preheat oven to 400°F. Melt 4 tablespoons butter in a saucepan and stir in flour. Cook over moderate heat for about 1 minute, then whisk in warm milk. Cook on low heat, stirring frequently, for 10 minutes. Season with salt, pepper and nutmeg.

Remove from heat and whisk a little sauce into egg yolks to warm them. Gradually whisk yolk mixture into sauce. Stir in Parmesan cheese. Beat egg whites until they hold firm peaks. Stir about a fifth of egg whites into sauce to lighten it, then fold in the remainder just until whites are incorporated.

Pour mixture into prepared pan and spread evenly across with a spatula. Bake until soufflé is puffed and lightly browned on top, about 15 minutes. Remove from oven and set aside to cool. It will flatten as it cools. Meanwhile, make the filling.

To prepare the filling, remove stems from spinach and wash leaves well in two changes of water. Set aside.

Using a 12-inch frying pan, cook onion and marjoram in oil over medium heat, stirring often until lightly browned and soft, about 10 minutes. In several batches, add spinach leaves with water clinging to the leaves. Season with salt and pepper. Cook just until tender and wilted, then remove to a colander. Press out as much liquid as possible, reserving it for pepper sauce.

Chop spinach very finely either by hand or in a food processor, without letting it become puree. Let cool.

Turn out soufflé onto another piece of parchment or waxed paper and remove the paper liner. Sprinkle Gruyère cheese over the surface, then spread spinach mixture evenly on top. Gently but tightly roll up soufflé, working from the long end of the roulade. Wrap in plastic wrap and refrigerate until ready to bake.

Brush roulade with milk or light cream to keep it from drying out. Bake at 400°F for 12 to 15 minutes, or until roulade is hot inside.

To serve, ladle 3 tablespoons Red Pepper Sauce on 6 plates, slice roulade into sixths and set each piece in the middle of the plate. Garnish with basil.

HELPFUL HINTS:

- *For best results, bring eggs to room temperature before preparing soufflé. If you've forgotten to set them out, cover them with hot water for 5 minutes, then drain.*

- *You may bake, fill and roll soufflé the night before. Wrap it tightly in plastic wrap and refrigerate until ready to use.*

Per Serving: 381 Calories; 22g Protein; 25g Fat; 19g Carbohydrates; 233mg Cholesterol; 664mg Sodium; 5g Fiber.

Red Pepper Sauce

This sauce makes a delicious and colorful addition to the Spinach Roulade.

MAKES 13 SERVINGS
(2½ CUPS)

3 large red peppers
Oil for brushing peppers
2 tablespoons olive oil
1 onion, minced
1½ teaspoons dried basil
½ teaspoon dried marjoram
½ teaspoon salt
½ cup white wine
½ cup tomato puree
2 cups water (or liquid from spinach plus water to make 2 cups)
1 tablespoon tomato paste
2 to 3 teaspoons white wine vinegar
1 tablespoon butter
2 tablespoons chopped fresh basil

Preheat broiler to 400°F. Cut peppers in half lengthwise, remove seeds and press open to flatten. Brush skins with oil. Place peppers skin side up in broiler until lightly charred, about 10 minutes. Remove, stacking on top of each other to create steam. Let stand 10 minutes, then remove as much charred skin as possible. (Don't rinse peppers under water or you'll lose much of their flavor.) Slice into strips.

Heat 2 tablespoons olive oil in a skillet. Sauté peppers, onion, basil, marjoram and salt for 5 minutes, stirring frequently. Add wine and cook until mixture is reduced to a sauce. Add tomato puree, water and tomato paste. Turn heat to low and simmer for 25 minutes. Puree thoroughly in a food processor, then pass through a food mill if possible. Return to skillet and cook at a low simmer. Season to taste with vinegar. Stir in butter and basil. Serve warm.

Per Serving: 53 Calories; 1g Protein; 3g Fat; 5g Carbohydrates; 3mg Cholesterol; 103mg Sodium; 0g Fiber.

Braised Seitan Roll with Apricots and Turnips

Although this recipe may seem intimidating at first, it is actually quite easy; the trickiest part is tying the roll. You can make the seitan several days in advance, then assemble and cook the roll a couple of hours before serving it. Serve it over a bed of wild or basmati rice. Leftovers make great sandwiches.

MAKES 6 SERVINGS

SEITAN
2$\frac{1}{2}$ cups full-bodied stock (replace $\frac{1}{4}$ cup with dry red wine if desired)
2 to 4 tablespoons soy sauce
$\frac{1}{4}$ teaspoon cayenne pepper
$\frac{1}{2}$ teaspoon garlic powder
About 3 cups gluten flour
2 to 3 tablespoons vegetable oil

BRAISING LIQUID
1 large turnip, diced
1 bunch green onions, chopped
4 ounces dried apricots, chopped (about 1 cup)
3 cups vegetable stock
1$\frac{1}{2}$ cups dry red wine
2 to 4 tablespoons soy sauce
1 carrot, diced
2 stalks celery, sliced
1 leek, sliced
1 teaspoon black peppercorns
$\frac{1}{2}$ teaspoon dried thyme
4 to 5 cloves garlic
2 tablespoons cornstarch or arrowroot powder
2 tablespoons water

To make the seitan, combine stock, soy sauce, cayenne and garlic powder in a bowl. Stir in about 2$\frac{1}{2}$ cups gluten flour. Add remaining gluten flour a little at a time until mixture congeals but is pliable and very soft. (You may need a little less or a little more than 3 cups.)

Roll or pat out into a rectangle about $\frac{1}{3}$ to $\frac{1}{2}$ inch thick. Heat oil in a nonstick skillet and cook seitan on both sides over medium-low heat until nicely browned. It will be firm and easy to handle.

To make the braising liquid, place turnip, green onions and apricots on the seitan and roll up tightly. Wrap string around the roll to hold it together tightly. Place in a Dutch oven with remaining ingredients except cornstarch or arrowroot and water. Cover and simmer for 45 minutes, occasionally basting the roll (which will expand during cooking). Remove roll and take off the string.

Strain liquid through a sieve or colander, pressing as much juice out of the vegetables as possible. Return liquid to the pot and reheat; discard vegetables. Dissolve cornstarch or arrowroot in water and add to the pot to thicken stock. To serve, slice roll into ½-inch-thick slices and place on a platter, or serve on individual plates over a bed of wild or basmati rice and pour sauce around it.

📌 Per Serving: 424 Calories; 36g Protein; 7g Fat; 49g Carbohydrates; 0mg Cholesterol; 657mg Sodium; 4g Fiber.

Harvest Vegetable Pie

The success of this layered vegetable pie depends upon making sure all ingredients are as dry as possible, so don't stint on cooking times. You can make the four filling ingredients a day ahead and store them in the refrigerator in plastic bags with a clean, folded paper towel tucked in to absorb any excess liquid. Fresh spinach has a much better flavor than frozen. One 12-inch nonstick skillet can be used to prepare all ingredients; simply rinse with hot water and dry in between.

MAKES 8 SERVINGS

Two 28-ounce cans whole tomatoes in tomato juice
1 clove garlic, minced
2 tablespoons tomato paste
Three 10-ounce bags washed, ready-to-eat salad spinach or three 10-ounce
    packages frozen chopped spinach, thawed
½ teaspoon freshly grated nutmeg
1 teaspoon each salt and freshly ground black pepper, divided
2 pounds mushrooms, stems included, cleaned
4 cups thinly sliced yellow onions
1 teaspoon sugar
1 cup crumbled feta cheese
4 eggs, beaten
10 sheets phyllo dough
1 cup grated part-skim mozzarella cheese

In a large colander or sieve set over a bowl, drain tomatoes. Save juice, covered and refrigerated, for later use. Cut tomatoes in half; place cut side down in colander and drain well. Squeeze seeds out of cut halves. Chop each tomato half into 8 pieces.

Place tomatoes in a lightly oiled 12-inch nonstick skillet. Sauté over high heat, stirring, until all juices have evaporated, about 5 minutes. Add garlic; cook, stirring, until garlic is soft, about 3 minutes. Add tomato paste; stir gently to combine. Cook until no juice remains, about 5 minutes. Turn tomato mixture onto a large plate lined with paper towels to cool.

Cook spinach in batches with 1 cup water in skillet, covered, over high heat until spinach wilts, about 5 minutes. Remove to colander to drain and cool. Squeeze spinach by handfuls until very dry. (If using frozen, thawed, chopped spinach, skip the cooking step and squeeze until no more moisture can be extracted.)

Chop spinach finely with a knife on a cutting board. Return to colander to drain. Squeeze a second time. In a medium bowl, mix spinach with nutmeg, ½ teaspoon salt and ½ teaspoon black pepper. Place on a paper-towel-lined plate.

Trim woody ends from mushroom stems. In a food processor, using shredding blade, shred mushrooms finely in batches. Or mince in batches on cutting board with knife. In a lightly oiled skillet over high heat, sauté mushrooms, stirring, until all moisture evaporates, up to 20 minutes. Season with remaining ½ teaspoon salt and ½ teaspoon black pepper. Turn onto paper-towel-lined plate to cool.

In lightly oiled skillet, sauté onions with sugar, stirring, until onions are caramelized but not burned, about 20 minutes. Turn out onto paper-towel-lined plate to cool.

At this point, the 4 filling ingredients may be put into separate self-seal plastic bags, each with a folded paper towel and refrigerated.

To assemble pie, preheat oven to 350°F. In a medium-sized bowl, mix together feta, eggs and spinach.

Unfold phyllo sheets. Lay sheets flat on length of waxed paper and cover top completely with a clean damp towel. Lightly oil a 10-inch springform pan. (Used for cheesecakes, a springform pan is the type with removable sides.)

Remove one sheet of phyllo from top. Cover remaining sheets with damp towel. Working from edges toward the center, spray or brush phyllo sheet lightly with olive oil or butter-flavored vegetable oil. Ease sheet into bottom of springform pan. Pat dough against sides; let excess hang out over pan edge. Repeat with second sheet at an angle to first sheet. Repeat with third and fourth sheets at angles so all four quarters of pan are covered.

Layer in 4 additional oiled sheets. Oil both sides of another sheet of phyllo; fold in half and ease into bottom of pan.

Add fillings in layers as follows: spinach-feta-eggs mixture; mushrooms, ½ cup mozzarella; tomatoes, ½ cup mozzarella; onions. Bring phyllo sheets up over top of pie. Spray lightly with oil.

Lightly oil another phyllo sheet. Cut in fourths, cutting along short side of rectangle. Fold each piece in half lengthwise. Roll up loosely, jelly-roll fashion. Pinch at bottom to make a rose and spread side slightly to form petals. Repeat with each piece. Place 4 phyllo roses in center of pie, pinching phyllo top to attach.

Place springform pan on baking sheet to catch any drips. Bake until phyllo is golden brown and filling is completely cooked, about 1 hour.

Remove from oven. Let sit 10 minutes. With a small, thin spatula, loosen phyllo from pan sides. Unclasp springform; remove sides. Lift pie onto serving plate leaving springform bottom in place. Garnish edges with flat-leaf parsley. Carve with a very sharp serrated knife.

VARIATIONS:

- *Omit eggs and feta in spinach layer and substitute $1/2$ cup shredded mozzarella-type soy cheese and 10-ounce package Japanese-style firm silken tofu that has been drained and pressed to extract moisture. In the tomato and mushroom layers, substitute $1/2$ cup soy mozzarella for dairy cheese.*

- *Instead of phyllo, try puff pastry. Use 2 sheets (1 package) frozen puff pastry, thawed according to package directions. Roll 1 sheet out slightly on a lightly floured surface. Cut into 3 equal short lengths. Fit each length into sides of springform pan, allowing top edges to hang out over sides. Seal edges with water. Save scraps.*

    Roll out second sheet slightly. Cut a circle $1/2$-inch larger than pan bottom. Save scraps. Ease circle into pan bottom, sealing edges to sides on inner side with water.

    Layer fillings as directed. Bring up overhanging puff pastry sides over top. Center will be open. Gather scraps; knead briefly to combine. Roll out into a 9-inch circle. Brush edges with water to seal. Place on top of pie. Cut decorative slits with a sharp knife. Bake at 400°F for 1 hour.

- *For simple phyllo pie, lay phyllo sheets as directed on 12-inch flat pizza pan. Layer fillings to within 1 inch of edge. Gather ends of phyllo together on top of pie and twist. Bake as directed.*

Per Serving: 339 Calories; 21g Protein; 13g Fat; 35g Carbohydrates; 139mg Cholesterol; 1032mg Sodium; 7g Fiber.

Vegetarian Tourtiére
(Quebec "Meat" Pie)

Tourtiére is usually made with a double crust, but using only a top crust lowers the fat. If you prefer, double the crust recipe and make it the traditional way.

MAKES 8 SERVINGS

LOW-FAT OIL PASTRY
$^1/_2$ cup whole-wheat flour
$^1/_2$ cup minus 1 tablespoon white pastry flour
$^3/_8$ teaspoon salt
$^3/_8$ teaspoon baking powder
$^3/_8$ teaspoon sugar
3 tablespoons canola oil
3 tablespoons curdled soymilk (see Note) or buttermilk

FILLING
1 large onion, minced
2 large cloves garlic, minced or crushed
1 pound seitan, drained and cut into chunks
$^1/_2$ cup hot water mixed with 2 teaspoons yeast extract or 1 vegetable bouillon cube
2 tablespoons ketchup
$1^1/_2$ teaspoons dried savory
$^1/_2$ teaspoon celery seed
$^1/_4$ teaspoon dried allspice
$^1/_2$ pound russet potatoes, peeled, boiled and coarsely mashed, or 1 cup
    instant mashed potato flakes mixed with $^2/_3$ cup boiling water
Soymilk for brushing

To make low-fat oil pastry, heat oven to 350°F. In a medium bowl, mix flours, salt, baking powder and sugar. Whisk together oil and curdled soymilk or buttermilk until well blended. Pour into flour mixture; mix gently with a fork until it holds together in a ball. If it is too dry, sprinkle with water. Place in a covered bowl in refrigerator while preparing filling. Makes one 9-inch crust.

To make filling, in a large nonstick skillet over high heat, sauté onions and garlic, adding a little water to prevent sticking. When onions are soft, pour into a large bowl.

Grind seitan in a food processor or food grinder. Mix with onion mixture, hot water–yeast extract mixture or bouillon, ketchup and seasonings. Add potatoes; mix well.

Lightly oil a 9-inch pie pan; press seitan mixture firmly into pan. Roll out pastry on a lightly floured surface. Fit it over filling, crimping edges attractively. Cut several slits in pastry. If you have scraps, cut leaves or other decorations; affix to crust with soymilk.

Brush pastry lightly with soymilk; bake 50 minutes. Tourtiére is traditionally served hot or cold with ketchup or tomato relish, but it's also good with chutney or vegetarian gravy.

NOTE: *To curdle soymilk, mix it with 1/2 teaspoon lemon juice. Do not use other nondairy "milks" when making pastry—only soymilk curdles like buttermilk when fresh lemon juice is added.*

HELPFUL HINT: *If you are in a hurry and not concerned about fat (the filling contains none), use a vegetarian pie crust mix or frozen pie crust.*

Per Serving: 207 Calories; 18g Protein; 6g Fat; 22g Carbohydrates; 0mg Cholesterol; 269mg Sodium; 3g Fiber.

15-Bean and Winter Squash Chili

This stick-to-your-ribs chili explodes the myth that vegetarian food leaves one feeling hungry.

MAKES 6 SERVINGS

1 cup 15-bean mixture, soaked overnight and drained (see Note)
7 cups water
1 tablespoon canola oil
1 large red onion, diced
1 large green or red bell pepper, seeded and diced
2 stalks celery, diced
2 or 3 cloves garlic, minced
2 cups peeled and diced butternut squash
15-ounce can stewed tomatoes
$\frac{1}{4}$ cup tomato paste
1 tablespoon dried oregano
1 to 2 tablespoons chili powder
$1\frac{1}{2}$ teaspoons ground cumin
1 teaspoon freshly ground black pepper
1 teaspoon salt

In a large saucepan, combine 15-bean mixture and water; bring to a simmer. Cook uncovered over medium-low heat, stirring occasionally, until beans are tender, about 1½ hours. Drain; reserve 3 cups cooking liquid.

In another large saucepan, heat oil. Add onion, bell pepper, celery and garlic; sauté 5 to 7 minutes. Stir in cooked beans, cooking liquid, squash, stewed tomatoes, tomato paste and seasonings. Cook 30 minutes over low heat, stirring occasionally. Remove from heat, cover and let stand 5 to 10 minutes before serving.

Ladle chili into bowls. Serve with warm French or Italian bread if desired.

NOTE: *15-bean mixtures are available packaged in supermarkets and health food stores. If you prefer, make your own by combining equal amounts dried black-eyed peas, red kidney beans, white kidney (cannellini) beans, green lentils, split peas, black beans, yellow split peas, navy beans, cranberry (Roman, shell or shellout) beans, great Northern beans, pinto beans, small white limas, red lentils, cow peas (field peas) and pink beans. Avoid using beans such as garbanzos and large lima beans, as these take longer to cook than other varieties.*

Per Serving: 215 Calories; 10g Protein; 3g Fat; 41g Carbohydrates; 0mg Cholesterol; 578mg Sodium; 11g Fiber.

Butternut Squash Tarts

For this tart, phyllo dough is rolled and gathered to make a crisp, brown frame around the colorful filling. When working with phyllo, remember to keep it covered with sheets of plastic wrap or waxed paper and a slightly damp towel to prevent it from drying out.

MAKES 8 TARTS

FILLING
2 pounds butternut squash, peeled and cubed
Salt to taste
1 small bunch fresh spinach, chopped, or ½ of a 10-ounce package
    frozen chopped spinach
⅓ cup dried currants, soaked in hot water 10 minutes and drained
½ teaspoon freshly grated nutmeg
¾ teaspoon salt
Freshly ground black pepper to taste

TART
Eight 18-by-14-inch sheets phyllo dough
¼ to ⅓ cup canola, safflower or sunflower oil
Dried Cranberry Sauce (recipe follows)

To make the filling, sprinkle cubed squash with salt, and steam until tender, about 15 minutes. Transfer to a large bowl and mash with 2 tablespoons cooking water; set aside. Cook spinach in a little water until tender. Drain, cool, squeeze out excess water and add to squash with drained currants, nutmeg and salt and pepper to taste. Mix well, or process in a food processor until smooth.

To assemble, preheat oven to 400°F. Place 1 sheet phyllo on work surface and brush lightly with oil. Place second sheet on top of first and brush with oil; continue until you have a stack of 4 sheets. Using scissors, trim 4 inches from length of phyllo sheets to make a square; reserve trimmed dough. Cut square into four 7- by-7-inch squares. Do this twice to get 8 squares.

Pack a ⅓-cup measure with squash filling; unmold in the center of one 7-inch-square stack of phyllo. Fold one reserved trimmed piece of phyllo in half lengthwise and wrap it around molded squash filling, gathering it slightly. Roll up each corner of the square to meet the filling and round off any corners by rolling them up. A crinkled effect makes the tart more attractive after it is baked.

Flatten tarts a little by pressing down with palm of hand, then brush with a little oil. Repeat until all filling and phyllo have been used. Bake on a greased baking sheet until phyllo is crisp and browned, about 10 to 15 minutes. Serve immediately with Dried Cranberry Sauce.

🍂 Per Tart (with ¼ Cup Sauce): 241 Calories; 4g Protein; 8g Fat; 36g Carbohydrates; 0mg Cholesterol; 333mg Sodium; 2g Fiber.

Dried Cranberry Sauce

This sauce imparts a wine and berry flavor that's a lovely accompaniment to the Butternut Squash Tarts.

MAKES 8 SERVINGS
(2 CUPS)

1 cup dried cranberries
1 cup red wine
1 cup water
¼ cup maple syrup
1 tablespoon cornstarch dissolved in 2 tablespoons water

Combine cranberries, wine, water and syrup in a saucepan; bring to a boil and simmer 5 minutes. Stir in cornstarch mixture and simmer an additional 5 minutes.

Per Serving: 50 Calories; 0g Protein; 0g Fat; 8g Carbohydrates; 0mg Cholesterol; 2mg Sodium; 1g Fiber.

Posole Casserole with Beets, Sweet Potatoes and Cornmeal Crust

Posole is a Native American stew of hominy, vegetables and herbs.

Makes 8 servings

POSOLE
1 tablespoon canola oil
1 medium onion, chopped
1 green bell pepper, diced
2 cloves garlic, minced
2 cups peeled and diced beets
3 cups water
½ cup pearl barley
2 cups diced, unpeeled sweet potatoes
15-ounce can hominy, drained and rinsed
1 tablespoon dried oregano
1 tablespoon chili powder
¼ teaspoon salt
½ teaspoon freshly ground black pepper
3 tablespoons tomato paste

CRUST
1 cup fine yellow cornmeal
1 cup unbleached white flour
2 tablespoons brown sugar
2 teaspoons baking powder
½ teaspoon salt
1 egg, beaten
1 cup buttermilk
1 tablespoon canola oil
⅓ cup shredded Gouda or provolone cheese (optional)

To make the posole, heat oil in a large saucepan; add onion, bell pepper and garlic. Sauté about 7 minutes. Add beets, water and barley; cook 10 minutes more over medium heat. Add potatoes, hominy, oregano, chili powder, salt and pepper; cook 25 minutes more, stirring occasionally. Remove from heat and stir in tomato paste. Keep warm.

To make the crust, preheat oven to 375°F. Mix together cornmeal, flour, sugar, baking powder and salt in a bowl. In a separate bowl, whisk together egg, buttermilk and oil. Gently fold liquid ingredients into dry ingredients until mixture forms a batter.

Pour batter into a lightly greased 9-by-13-inch baking pan. Spread posole over crust. Sprinkle cheese over top, if desired.

Bake until top is lightly browned, about 25 minutes. Remove from oven and let stand 10 minutes before serving.

🍂 Per Serving: 411 Calories; 14g Protein; 10g Fat; 67g Carbohydrates; 45mg Cholesterol; 658mg Sodium; 7g Fiber.

Autumn Risotto with Squash and Spinach

Risotto is a creamy rice dish made with arborio rice, an Italian grain. Butternut squash melds smoothly into the risotto and delivers a wave of warm autumn flavors. Spinach and corn add a splash of color as well as taste.

MAKES 6 SERVINGS

1 to 2 tablespoons olive oil
1 medium onion, diced
12 large mushrooms, sliced
2 cloves garlic, minced
2 cups peeled and diced butternut squash (about 2 small squash)
2 cups arborio rice
4 cups water
1 cup diced carrots
$\frac{1}{2}$ teaspoon freshly ground white pepper
$\frac{1}{2}$ to 1 teaspoon salt, or to taste
1 cup corn kernels
2 cups chopped fresh spinach
$\frac{1}{4}$ cup freshly grated Parmesan cheese
2 tablespoons minced fresh parsley

In a large nonstick saucepan or Dutch oven, heat oil; add onion, mushrooms and garlic. Sauté until mushrooms are very limp and onions are soft, about 7 minutes. Add squash, rice, 2 cups water, carrots, pepper and salt; cook uncovered over medium-low heat about 10 minutes, stirring frequently.

Add remaining 2 cups water, corn and spinach; cook, stirring frequently, until water is absorbed and rice is tender, about 10 minutes. Turn off heat and stir in cheese. Transfer risotto to a large serving bowl and sprinkle parsley on top.

🍂 Per Serving: 468 Calories; 11g Protein; 5g Fat; 68g Carbohydrates; 3mg Cholesterol; 302mg Sodium; 3g Fiber.

Vegetable Quinoa Bake with Red Kuri Squash

Quinoa, an ancient grain with a nutty flavor and chewy texture, teams up with red kuri, a pumpkin-like squash with a bright, reddish-orange flesh and thin skin. (If red kuri is unavailable, try butternut squash or pumpkin.) Serve with crunchy green vegetables such as broccoli, brussels sprouts or asparagus.

MAKES 6 SERVINGS

1 tablespoon canola oil
1 medium onion, chopped
8 to 10 mushrooms, sliced
1 large bell pepper, diced
1 jalapeño pepper, seeded and minced (optional)
1 small zucchini, diced
2 cloves garlic, minced
3 cups water
1^1/$_2$ cups quinoa
2 cups peeled and diced red kuri, pumpkin or other winter squash
1 cup chopped kale or escarole
2 tablespoons fresh minced parsley (or 1 tablespoon dried parsley)
^{1}/$_2$ teaspoon salt
^{1}/$_2$ teaspoon freshly ground black pepper

Preheat oven to 400°F. In a saucepan, heat oil over medium heat; add onion, mushrooms, peppers, zucchini and garlic. Sauté about 5 to 7 minutes. Stir in remaining ingredients and bring to a boil.

Transfer mixture to a 9-by-13-inch casserole dish and cover. Bake until liquid is absorbed, about 35 to 40 minutes.

Remove from oven and fluff with a fork. Let stand 5 minutes before serving.

 Per Serving: 167 Calories; 6g Protein; 4g Fat; 29g Carbohydrates; 0mg Cholesterol; 166mg Sodium; 4g Fiber.

Baked Pumpkin with Vegetable Pilaf

For far too long, pumpkins have been typecast as either pie filling or porch ornaments. When baked and stuffed, a pumpkin makes a magnificent centerpiece.

MAKES 4 SERVINGS

One 5- to 6-pound pumpkin or other winter squash (see Note)
1 tablespoon canola oil
1 small onion, diced
1 red bell pepper, seeded and diced
1 small jalapeño pepper, seeded and minced
1 small zucchini, diced (about 1$\frac{1}{2}$ cups)
2 tablespoons minced shallots
1$\frac{1}{2}$ cups brown rice
$\frac{1}{4}$ cup raisins
$\frac{1}{2}$ teaspoon freshly ground black pepper
$\frac{1}{4}$ teaspoon turmeric
$\frac{1}{4}$ teaspoon salt
3 cups water
8 medium broccoli florets, blanched
2 tablespoons minced fresh cilantro (optional)

To cook pumpkin, preheat oven to 375°F. With a sharp knife, cut a 4-inch lid off top of pumpkin. (Cut at an angle so lid goes back on more easily.) With a large spoon, scoop out seeds and stringy fibers; discard or reserve for another use. Cover hole with a sheet of foil and set pumpkin lid back on top. Place in a baking pan with ½ inch water; bake until inside is tender, 50 minutes to 1 hour. Remove from oven and keep warm.

To make the pilaf, heat oil in a large saucepan. Add onion, peppers, zucchini and shallots. Sauté until vegetables are tender, about 7 minutes. Stir in rice, raisins, black pepper, turmeric and salt; cook 1 minute more. Add water; cover and cook over medium-low heat until liquid is absorbed, about 45 minutes. Fluff pilaf with a fork and stir in broccoli. Stir in cilantro if desired. Spoon pilaf into pumpkin and cover with lid. (Discard foil.)

Set stuffed pumpkin on a large platter in center of table. When serving pilaf, scrape inside of pumpkin with serving spoon and mix pumpkin into pilaf.

NOTE: *If you double recipe, use 2 pumpkins, not 1 large pumpkin.*

Per Serving: 398 Calories; 15g Protein; 6g Fat; 90g Carbohydrates; 0mg Cholesterol; 200mg Sodium; 13g Fiber.

Wild and Brown Rice with Leeks, Asparagus and Corn

Brown rice and wild rice are combined with vegetables for a straight-from-the-hearth meal. Asparagus, frozen if you can't find fresh, endows the dish with a dash of panache.

MAKES 4 SERVINGS

1½ tablespoons olive oil
2 cups sliced leeks (about 2 large)
1 medium zucchini, diced (about 2 cups)
3 or 4 cloves garlic, minced
½ teaspoon turmeric
4 cups water
1½ cups long-grain brown rice
½ cup wild rice
2 medium carrots, diced
1 cup fresh or frozen green peas
2 ears corn, cut into 1-inch sections
2 tablespoons minced fresh parsley (or 1 tablespoon dried parsley)
½ teaspoon dried thyme
½ teaspoon freshly ground black pepper
½ teaspoon salt
12 stalks frozen or fresh asparagus, trimmed and peeled

Preheat oven to 375°F. In a large cast-iron skillet or Dutch oven, heat oil; add leeks, zucchini and garlic. Cook over medium heat about 7 minutes, stirring occasionally. Add turmeric; cook 1 minute more. Stir in water, brown rice, wild rice, carrots, peas, corn, parsley, thyme, pepper and salt. Cover and bake 45 minutes.

Remove from oven and fluff with a fork. Arrange asparagus over top, cover and bake until liquid is absorbed, about 10 to 15 minutes. Remove from oven; let stand 10 minutes. Serve from skillet if desired.

Per Serving: 210 Calories; 7g Protein; 5g Fat; 91g Carbohydrates; 0mg Cholesterol; 295mg Sodium; 6g Fiber.

Pumpkin Curry with Lentils and Apples

Tired of baking every Thanksgiving? You can make this main course on the stovetop. For an artful presentation, serve inside a hollowed-out pumpkin (see Baked Pumpkin with Vegetable Pilaf, page 95). A yogurt-cucumber sauce (raita) makes a soothing accompaniment.

MAKES 6 SERVINGS

1 cup red or brown lentils
6 cups water
$^{1}/_{2}$ teaspoon turmeric
1 tablespoon canola oil
1 large onion, diced
2 tomatoes, cored and chopped
3 to 4 cloves garlic, minced
$1^{1}/_{2}$ tablespoons curry powder
2 teaspoon ground cumin
$^{1}/_{2}$ teaspoon freshly ground black pepper
$^{1}/_{2}$ teaspoon salt
$^{1}/_{4}$ teaspoon ground cloves
2 cups peeled and chopped pumpkin or other winter squash
2 cups chopped, unpeeled white potatoes (about 2 medium)
8 medium cauliflower florets
2 medium carrots, peeled and diced (about 1 cup)
2 cups shredded leafy greens (kale, escarole or spinach)
2 apples, unpeeled, cored and diced
Cooked basmati or jasmine rice

Place lentils, water and turmeric in a saucepan; cook about 45 minutes over medium-low heat. Drain, reserving 2½ cups cooking liquid.

Heat oil in large saucepan; add onion. Sauté over medium heat 4 minutes. Add tomatoes and garlic; cook 4 minutes more, stirring occasionally. Add curry, cumin, pepper, salt and cloves; cook 1 minute more, stirring frequently.

Stir in lentils, reserved cooking liquid, and pumpkin, potatoes, cauliflower and carrots; cook over medium-low heat until vegetables are tender, 35 to 45 minutes. Stir in greens and apples; cook about 15 minutes more, stirring occasionally.

Transfer to a large serving bowl and serve with basmati or jasmine rice.

Per Serving: 285 Calories; 14g Protein; 4g Fat; 54g Carbohydrates; 0mg Cholesterol; 233mg Sodium; 17g Fiber.

Succotash-Stuffed Butternut Squash

Succotash, the traditional Native American dish of corn, lima beans and spices, fills the squash with the muted colors and flavors of autumn.

MAKES 4 SERVINGS

2 medium butternut squash
2 cups frozen baby lima beans, thawed
1 tablespoon canola oil
1 medium red or yellow onion, diced
2 red or green bell peppers, diced
1 jalapeño pepper, seeded and minced (optional)
2 cloves garlic, minced
2 cups fresh or frozen corn kernels
1½ to 3 teaspoons dried oregano, or to taste
½ teaspoon dried thyme
½ teaspoon freshly ground black pepper
¼ teaspoon freshly grated nutmeg
¼ teaspoon salt
¼ cup bread crumbs
¼ cup freshly grated Parmesan cheese

Preheat oven to 350°F. Cut squash in half lengthwise. Scoop out seeds and stringy fibers; discard. Place squash cut-side down on a sheet pan with ¼ inch water. Bake 35 to 40 minutes, until flesh is easily pierced with a fork. Remove from oven, turn squash over, drain water and let squash cool for a few minutes.

Meanwhile, place lima beans in boiling water to cover; cook 10 minutes. Drain in a colander and cool slightly.

Heat oil in a saucepan; add onion, peppers and garlic. Sauté 5 to 7 minutes. Add lima beans, corn, oregano, thyme, black pepper, nutmeg and salt; cook over low heat 5 minutes more, stirring occasionally. Remove from heat; keep warm.

When squash is cool, carefully scoop out flesh from shells, coarsely chop and blend into lima bean mixture. Spoon mixture back into shells and sprinkle with bread crumbs and cheese.

Place stuffed squash under a hot broiler 5 to 7 minutes, until lightly browned. Present stuffed squash on large serving platters at table.

Per Serving: 291 Calories; 12g Protein; 6g Fat; 53g Carbohydrates; 4mg Cholesterol; 507mg Sodium; 8g Fiber.

Buttercup Squash, Parsnip and Cranberry Bean Stew

The mildly sweet flavor and firm texture of parsnips pairs well with the delicately flavored buttercup squash; chipotle pepper adds a smoky, peppery nuance.

MAKES 4 SERVINGS

1 tablespoon canola oil
1 cup sliced celery (about 2 medium stalks)
2 or 3 garlic cloves, minced
1 chipotle pepper, minced
4 large tomatoes, cored and diced
1½ tablespoons paprika
1 tablespoon dried oregano
Salt and freshly ground black pepper to taste
2 cups peeled and diced buttercup or butternut squash
2 cups peeled and diced parsnips (about 2 large)
12 to 16 pearl onions, peeled
1 cup diced carrots
2½ cups water
1½ cups cooked or canned cranberry beans, drained
1 cup fresh or frozen corn kernels
8 broccoli florets

In a large saucepan, heat oil; add celery, garlic and chipotle. Sauté 3 to 4 minutes. Add tomatoes, paprika, oregano, salt and pepper; cook about 8 minutes more over medium-low heat, stirring frequently, until mixture resembles thick pulp.

Add squash, parsnips, onions, carrots and water; cook, stirring occasionally, until squash and parsnips are tender, about 30 minutes. Stir in beans, corn and broccoli. Cover and cook 5 to 10 minutes more.

Serve in a large bowl with brown rice or quinoa on the side, or in a baked pumpkin (see Baked Pumpkin with Vegetable Pilaf, page 95).

 Per Serving: 237 Calories; 7g Protein; 5g Fat; 50g Carbohydrates; 0mg Cholesterol; 68mg Sodium; 9g Fiber.

Vegetable Tagine with Olives and Prunes

Bake this stew for excellent results, as baked vegetables are more likely to stay whole and tender without getting mushy. For stovetop cooking, continue cooking over medium-low heat until vegetables are tender. Substitute your own favorite seasonal vegetables.

MAKES 6 SERVINGS

2 tablespoons olive oil
4 shallots, coarsely chopped
1 stalk celery, diced
1-inch piece peeled ginger, slivered
2 cloves garlic, slivered
1 cinnamon stick
1 teaspoon freshly ground black pepper
$1\frac{1}{2}$ teaspoons paprika
$1\frac{1}{2}$ teaspoons ground cumin
$1\frac{1}{2}$ teaspoons ground coriander
$\frac{1}{8}$ teaspoon cayenne pepper, or to taste
1 teaspoon salt
32-ounce can crushed or diced tomatoes
1 large carrot, peeled and cut into chunks
$\frac{1}{3}$ pound string beans, ends trimmed
1 small butternut squash or sweet potato, peeled and cut into chunks
$\frac{1}{2}$ head cauliflower, cut into florets
$\frac{1}{2}$ fennel bulb, trimmed and cut into chunks
Vegetable stock or water as needed (see Note)
$\frac{1}{4}$ teaspoon crushed saffron
1 cup cooked chickpeas
$\frac{1}{2}$ cup whole pitted Kalamata olives
$\frac{1}{2}$ cup halved pitted prunes
3 tablespoons chopped fresh parsley

Preheat oven to 350°F. Add oil to large stew pot; sauté shallots, celery, ginger, garlic and cinnamon stick over low heat until shallots and celery are soft, stirring frequently, about 7 minutes. Add black pepper, paprika, cumin, coriander, cayenne and salt. Cook, stirring, until spices are fragrant, about 1 minute.

Stir in tomatoes, carrot, string beans, squash or sweet potato, cauliflower and fennel. Add additional vegetable stock or water to cover vegetables. Add saffron. Spoon mixture into a large baking dish and bake, covered, until vegetables are tender, 40 to 45 minutes. About 5 minutes before stew is done, stir in chickpeas, olives and prunes. Add parsley before serving. If desired, spoon over couscous.

VARIATION: *For stovetop cooking, stir in tomatoes, carrot and string beans; cook until halfway done. Stir in squash or sweet potato, cauliflower and fennel; cook until crisp-tender. Proceed with recipe.*

NOTE: *The type of tomatoes used will determine the amount of stock or water needed to cook vegetables. Crushed tomatoes will require adding about 1 cup water to cook. Stovetop cooking may require slightly more water; diced tomatoes may not require as much water. The finished stew should be somewhat dry, not soupy, and vegetables tender but shapely, not soggy.*

Per Serving: 271 Calories; 10g Protein; 7g Fat; 49g Carbohydrates; 0mg Cholesterol; 1075mg Sodium; 10g Fiber.

Shiitake Pot Pie with Polenta Crust

Because the crust is made of polenta and not pastry, prep time in the kitchen is greatly reduced, as is the fat content. This dish will impress company.

MAKES 4 SERVINGS
(4 TO 6 CUPS)

FILLING
$^1\!/_2$ ounce dried porcini mushrooms
$^3\!/_4$ cup hot water
1 tablespoon plus $^1\!/_2$ teaspoon olive oil
2 pounds new potatoes, cubed
1 medium onion, diced
4 cloves garlic, crushed
1 pound shiitake mushrooms, stems removed and sliced
1 teaspoon dried thyme
$^1\!/_8$ teaspoon cayenne pepper
$1^1\!/_2$ tablespoons flour
1 cup peas

CRUST
3 cups water
$^1\!/_4$ teaspoon salt
$^3\!/_4$ cups polenta

Soak porcinis in ¾ cup hot water for at least an hour. Remove mushrooms from water and, depending on their quality, either discard or reserve for another use. Strain soaking water through cheesecloth, a fine sieve or a coffee filter. Set aside.

Preheat oven to 425°F. Lightly oil roasting pan large enough to hold potatoes in one layer. Roast potatoes, stirring once or twice to prevent sticking and to brown evenly, until tender, about 35 minutes. (The potatoes can be roasted several hours in advance or even the preceding day.)

While potatoes roast, heat ½ teaspoon of oil in a nonstick skillet. Add onion and garlic; sauté until onions are soft. Add shiitake mushrooms, thyme and cayenne; cook until mushrooms soften and shrink to about half their original size, about 15 minutes.

In a separate skillet, heat remaining oil. Make a roux by adding flour and stirring until flour begins to brown. Add roux and porcini water to mushroom mixture; cook until liquid reduces by about a third, about 5 minutes.

Remove potatoes from oven; reduce oven temperature to 350°F. Combine mushroom mixture, potatoes and peas in a 9-by-9-inch lightly oiled baking pan. Set aside.

For crust, bring water and salt to a rolling boil. Add polenta slowly, stirring constantly. Turn heat down to medium; stir constantly until mixture thickens and begins to pull away from sides of the pot, about 10 minutes.

Spread polenta over vegetable-and-mushroom mixture; bake until polenta begins to brown, about 15 minutes. Remove from oven and let sit 15 minutes before cutting.

Per Serving: 427 Calories; 12g Protein; 5g Fat; 86g Carbohydrates; 0mg Cholesterol; 154mg Sodium; 9g Fiber.

Cherokee Kanuchi Stew with Root Vegetables

Use hickory nuts if possible, as they provide the most authentic flavor. A mixture of hazelnuts and pecans is a good substitute.

MAKES 8 SERVINGS

1 cup pecans
1 cup hazelnuts
2 quarts water
2 cups chopped onion
1 pound carrots, cut into 1-inch pieces
8 ounces sunchokes (Jerusalem artichokes), scrubbed and sliced
    into $^1/_2$-inch pieces
1 pound sweet potatoes, peeled and cut into 1-inch cubes
1 cup canned hominy
2 cups frozen corn
2 cups fresh green beans, cut into 1-inch pieces
Salt and freshly ground black pepper to taste

Preheat oven to 350°F. Place pecans and hazelnuts on separate cookie sheets; bake 7 minutes. Remove as much skin as possible from the hazelnuts by rubbing with a terrycloth towel. Place immediately in a food processor or blender; grind to a paste. Add pecans; continue grinding.

Boil water. Add nuts, onion and carrots; simmer 30 minutes. Nut paste will rise to the surface; stir down occasionally. Add sunchokes, sweet potatoes, hominy and corn; simmer 30 minutes. Add green beans; simmer 15 minutes. Add salt and pepper.

This dish may be prepared 1 to 2 days ahead. Serve with cornbread.

Per Serving: 391 Calories; 8g Protein; 22g Fat; 50g Carbohydrates; 0mg Cholesterol; 213mg Sodium; 10g Fiber.

Mushroom-Pecan Stew

Any mixture of fresh or dried mushrooms will work in this recipe; fresh portobello, cèpe, morel and porcini are especially good. Don't use shiitake mushrooms; the flavor isn't quite right.

Makes 8 servings

1 cup finely ground toasted pecans
4 cups water
1 teaspoon salt
$^1/_2$ cup stone-ground cornmeal
3 tablespoons butter or vegetable oil
2 cups coarsely chopped onions
8 cups fresh mushrooms, chopped, or 8 ounces dried wild mushrooms,
    soaked, drained and chopped
$^1/_3$ cup fresh chives, minced

Stir pecans into boiling water. Add salt; simmer 5 minutes. Slowly stir in cornmeal; simmer 10 minutes.

While nut mixture cooks, heat oil or butter. Sauté onions on low heat until translucent. Sauté mushrooms with onions until they begin to brown and exude juices. Pour mushroom-onion mixture into nut mixture; simmer 15 minutes. Add chives. If desired, serve stew over fried cornmeal mush or soft polenta.

Per Serving: 201 Calories; 4g Protein; 15g Fat; 16g Carbohydrates; 12mg Cholesterol; 342mg Sodium; 3g Fiber.

Vegetarian Shepherd's Pie

This recipe lends itself to creativity. If you decide to experiment with different versions of the three components of the dish, use this formula as a guide: For 4 servings, use 4 cups vegetable hash, ½ cup gravy and 6 medium potatoes, cooked and mashed.

MAKES 4 SERVINGS

MASHED POTATOES
6 medium russet potatoes, peeled and quartered
½ cup buttermilk or as needed
2 tablespoons freshly grated Parmesan cheese
Salt and freshly ground black pepper to taste

SUN-DRIED TOMATO GRAVY
½ cup sun-dried tomatoes
⅔ cup water
2 teaspoons olive oil
1 medium onion, chopped
1 large green pepper, chopped
1 small red pepper, chopped
2 cloves garlic, minced
1 teaspoon dried basil
1 teaspoon dried oregano
½ teaspoon ground cumin
2 tablespoons soy sauce
½ cup dry textured vegetable protein granules
¾ cup water

HASH
1 teaspoon olive oil
1 large onion, chopped
2 medium carrots, chopped
2 to 4 tablespoons water
2 cups cooked lentils
2 cloves garlic, minced
½ teaspoon dried oregano
1 tablespoon Worcestershire sauce

GARNISHES (OPTIONAL)
2 tablespoons grated Cheddar cheese
Paprika

Boil potatoes in water to cover for 15 minutes, or until easily pierced with the tip of a paring knife. Drain potatoes and return to cooking pot. Shake potatoes over medium heat for a minute or two, until dry. Mash well, then stir in buttermilk and Parmesan. Season with salt and pepper.

To make the gravy, place tomatoes in a small pot and cover with ⅔ cup water. Bring to a simmer and cook, covered, for 5 minutes, or until softened. Remove tomatoes and chop, reserving cooking liquid.

In a medium-sized saucepan, heat oil over medium-high heat. Sauté onion, peppers and garlic until lightly browned, adding basil, oregano and cumin during cooking. Add tomatoes and their cooking liquid, soy sauce, TVP and ¾ cup water. Cover and simmer about 15 minutes.

To make hash, in a large saucepan, heat oil over medium-high heat. Sauté onion for 1 minute. Add carrots and water; sauté until onion is translucent and carrots are tender, about 8 minutes. Stir in lentils, garlic, oregano and Worcestershire sauce. Cook 1 or 2 minutes, then remove from heat.

To assemble, preheat oven to 350°F. Lightly butter a 2-quart gratin dish. Spread hash in dish, then spoon gravy over hash. Spread mashed potatoes over gravy. If desired, sprinkle with grated cheese and a dusting of paprika. Bake for 30 minutes, until bubbly and fragrant.

VARIATIONS:

- *Substitute potato cooking water for buttermilk in the mashed potatoes. Add a bit of olive oil; the fruitiness of the oil nicely complements the earthy flavor of the potatoes.*

- *A head of roasted garlic puree makes a mellow, aromatic addition to mashed potatoes.*

- *For a decorative touch, spoon or pipe mashed potatoes around outer edge of the dish, leaving the center open.*

Per Serving: 245 Calories; 12g Protein; 4g Fat; 45g Carbohydrates; 2mg Cholesterol; 662mg Sodium; 7g Fiber.

Sweet Rice, Butternut Squash and Ginger

Used mostly for sweet dishes in Asian cookery, sweet rice has a delicious taste and lends itself to aromatic flavors, warm spices and unusual vegetable combinations. This recipe can serve as a side dish or entree, preceded by a rich soup and accompanied by a green salad garnished with toasted nuts and a basket of whole-grain buns.

MAKES 10 SIDE-DISH SERVINGS
OR 5 MAIN-DISH SERVINGS

2 cups short-grain or medium-grain sweet rice
6 cups warm water
3 cups butternut squash, peeled and chopped in $\frac{1}{4}$-inch chunks
$\frac{1}{3}$ cup golden raisins
$\frac{1}{4}$ cup chopped scallions (white and green parts)
1 tablespoon finely grated fresh ginger
1 teaspoon salt
$\frac{3}{4}$ teaspoon cinnamon
$\frac{1}{2}$ teaspoon white pepper (preferably freshly ground)
1 tablespoon tamari

Combine rice and water in a large bowl; soak 4 hours, or cover, refrigerate and soak overnight.

Drain rice. In large bowl, combine rice with squash, raisins, scallions, ginger, salt, cinnamon and pepper; toss to mix well. Spread a layer of cheesecloth in an electric steamer or over 1 layer of a stackable metal or bamboo steamer. Cover rice mixture and steam over boiling water 30 minutes. Remove rice to a serving bowl; toss with tamari. Serve immediately.

VARIATION: *If sweet rice is not available, boil 2 cups jasmine or basmati rice 10 minutes with 2 cups water. Drain water and finish cooking rice in steamer with vegetables and seasonings.*

HELPFUL HINT: *Peel squash with a carrot peeler, then cut in half lengthwise, scoop out seeds and dice.*

◢ Per Side-Dish Serving: 176 Calories; 3g Protein; 0g Fat; 40g Carbohydrates; 0mg Cholesterol; 317mg Sodium; 2g Fiber.

◢ Per Main-Dish Serving: 352 Calories; 6g Protein; 0g Fat; 80g Carbohydrates; 0mg Cholesterol; 634mg Sodium; 4g Fiber.

Millet Loaf with Mushroom Sauce

This recipe offers a variation on meat loaf. It's especially tasty with a savory sauce.

MAKES 8 SERVINGS

1 tablespoon canola oil
1 onion, minced
2 cloves garlic, minced
1 cup cleaned and chopped mushrooms
2 tablespoons chopped fresh parsley
2 teaspoons minced fresh thyme
Salt to taste
1½ cups cooked millet
1½ cups cooked short-grain brown rice
3 egg whites or equivalent Egg Replacer
½ pound firm tofu, mashed
1 cup grated soy Cheddar cheese
Freshly ground black pepper to taste
Mushroom Sauce (recipe follows)

Preheat oven to 350°F. Heat oil in a medium saucepan over medium heat. Sauté onion until aromatic and soft, about 3 minutes. Add garlic, mushrooms, herbs and salt; cook 5 minutes, or until mushrooms exude liquid. Transfer mixture to a large bowl; add millet, rice, egg whites or Egg Replacer, tofu and soy cheese. Add pepper.

Lightly oil an 8-inch loaf pan and line with lightly oiled waxed paper. Spoon millet mixture into pan. Bake until golden, about 1¼ hours. Let loaf cool slightly before unmolding. Slice and serve with mushroom sauce.

Per Serving (with 2 Tablespoons Sauce): 198 Calories; 12g Protein; 6g Fat; 24g Carbohydrates; 0mg Cholesterol; 404mg Sodium; 2g Fiber.

Mushroom Sauce

Use this sauce to top off the Millet Loaf.

MAKES 3 CUPS
(48 TABLESPOONS)

2 tablespoons canola oil
2 tablespoons flour
2 cups vegetable broth
2 cups sliced sautéed mushrooms
$\frac{1}{2}$ tablespoon tomato paste
Salt and freshly ground black pepper to taste

Heat oil in a small saucepan over low heat. Add flour; cook 2 minutes, stirring constantly. Remove roux from heat and cool slightly. In a medium saucepan, bring broth to a boil. Whisk in roux; stir in mushrooms and tomato paste. Season with salt and pepper. Cook over low heat 20 minutes. Serve warm.

 Per 2 Tablespoons: 10 Calories; 1g Protein; 1g Fat; 1g Carbohydrate; 0mg Cholesterol; 18mg Sodium; 0g Fiber.

A HARVEST
of Side Dishes

Throughout most of the year, the side dish plays second fiddle to the main dish. While the entree fills the center of the plate and commands attention, the side dish is served, well, over on the side. However, the Thanksgiving supper is a virtual showcase for not just one, but several inviting side dishes. Bowls of mashed potatoes, candied yams, cranberry molds and baked squash rekindle the warm and fuzzy memories of Thanksgivings past. True, the main dish still basks in the glamour and the glory, but an assortment of side dishes can best symbolize the sumptuous spirit of the celebration.

From the traditional to the innovative, this chapter features an all-star team of alluring side dishes. There are recipes for familiar comfort foods, such as Paprika Mashed Potatoes and Baked Candied Sweet Potatoes, as well as more elaborate and exotic offerings, such as Royal Risotto with Asparagus and Artichokes and Stuffed Thanksgiving Pumpkins. These enticing recipes showcase the colors and flavors of autumn and add panache to the dinner table.

Since the early Thanksgivings, harvest favorites such as winter squash, beans, pumpkin and cranberries have appeared as faithful companions to the main dish. Seasonal side dishes expand the range of tastes and textures of the dinner and coax out the flavors of the entree. By offering a supporting cast of side dishes, you'll stay true to Thanksgiving's venerated roots and at the same time ensure that your holiday dinner is a winner. So get ready to pass the vegetable medley, make room for the squash and dish out the potatoes!

Perfect Mashed Potatoes

There are several secrets to perfect mashed potatoes. The first is to use only enough water to cover and to salt the water so no additional salt is needed. The second is to heat the liquids. The third, and most important, is to use a potato masher or ricer before whipping.

MAKES 6 SERVINGS

2 pounds (about 6 medium) russet potatoes
1 quart water
1 teaspoon salt
1 cup oat milk
1 tablespoon canola or extra-virgin olive oil
$^1/_2$ teaspoon white pepper, preferably freshly ground
Salt to taste

Peel potatoes, removing all eyes and blemishes. Halve potatoes lengthwise. Cut each half into eight similar-size pieces.

Place potatoes in a 3½- to 4-quart pan. Cover with 1 quart water. Add 1 teaspoon salt; cover pan. Over high heat bring water to a boil, about 10 minutes. Reduce heat to medium. Cook covered until potatoes are fork-tender, about 10 to 12 minutes.

Meanwhile, in a small saucepan over low heat, bring oat milk to a simmer. Do not boil.

Drain cooked potatoes. Return to pan and mash very well with an old-fashioned potato masher.

Scrape potatoes with a spatula into mixer bowl or a separate bowl. With whip attachment on medium speed or with hand mixer, begin to whip potatoes while slowly adding hot oat milk. Scrape bowl to incorporate all potatoes. Add oil and pepper. Whip to mix. Taste for salt, adding more if necessary.

Serve immediately or keep warm for up to 1 hour by putting bowl, covered, in a hot water bath.

Per Serving: 164 Calories; 3g Protein; 3g Fat; 33g Carbohydrates; 0mg Cholesterol; 410mg Sodium; 3g Fiber.

Soy Mashed Potatoes

This recipe has the rich, creamy flavor of traditional mashed potatoes but a lot less fat.

MAKES 8 SERVINGS
(4 CUPS)

1³⁄₄ pounds red-skinned potatoes, peeled and cut into 1-inch cubes
(about 5 cups)
1 cup soymilk or oat milk
2 tablespoons corn or canola oil
1¹⁄₄ teaspoons salt

Steam potatoes over simmering water until tender, about 15 minutes. Transfer potatoes to medium bowl. Add soymilk or oat milk, oil and salt, and mash until smooth. Serve right away.

🍂 Per Serving: 125 Calories; 3g Protein; 4g Fat; 20g Carbohydrates; 0mg Cholesterol; 372mg Sodium; 2g Fiber.

Mushroom Medley

This recipe is great with shiitake mushrooms or a mixture of shiitake, cremini and white button mushrooms.

MAKES 6 SERVINGS
(3 CUPS)

3 tablespoons extra-virgin olive oil
10 cloves garlic, minced
¹⁄₂ cup chopped fresh parsley
1 pound fresh mushroom caps, quartered
Salt and freshly ground black or white pepper to taste

In a large saucepan, heat oil over medium heat. Add garlic and parsley and cook, stirring often, 1 minute. Add mushrooms and toss over high heat just until beginning to soften, 1 to 2 minutes. Remove from heat and season with salt and pepper. Serve immediately.

🍂 Per Serving: 89 Calories; 2g Protein; 7g Fat; 6g Carbohydrates; 0mg Cholesterol; 57mg Sodium; 1g Fiber.

Royal Risotto with Asparagus and Artichokes

If there were a hall of fame for dishes, risotto would have to be a charter member. Asparagus and artichokes endow this classic rendition with regal flavors.

Makes 6 servings
(6 cups)

1 tablespoon olive oil
1 medium red onion, diced
10 to 12 white button mushrooms, sliced
4 cloves garlic, minced
4^1/$_2$ cups water
1^1/$_2$ cups arborio rice
^{1}/$_2$ cup dry white wine
^{1}/$_2$ teaspoon freshly ground white pepper
^{1}/$_2$ teaspoon salt
^{1}/$_2$ teaspoon ground turmeric
10 to 12 asparagus spears, trimmed and cut into 1-inch sections
14-ounce can artichoke hearts, rinsed and coarsely chopped
^{1}/$_2$ cup freshly grated Parmesan cheese

Heat oil in a large saucepan over medium heat. Add onion, mushrooms and garlic. Cook, stirring, for 6 minutes. Add 2 cups water, rice, wine and seasonings. Bring to a simmer; cook, uncovered, over medium-low heat, stirring frequently until most of the liquid is absorbed, about 10 minutes.

Stir in another 2 cups water, asparagus and artichokes. Bring to a simmer. Cook, stirring, until rice is al dente, about 12 to 14 minutes more. Adjust heat so rice doesn't burn on the bottom, and add remaining ½ cup of water if needed.

Remove from heat; let stand for a few minutes before serving. Fold in cheese.

HELPFUL HINT: *For an herbal nuance, sprinkle chopped fresh parsley or basil over the risotto at the last minute.*

Per Serving: 289 Calories; 9g Protein; 5g Fat; 48g Carbohydrates; 25mg Cholesterol; 489mg Sodium; 2g Fiber.

Wild Rice Pilaf with Ginger Dressing

Not only does this dish taste great, but it looks pretty as well. The fresh ginger dressing goes nicely with the nutty flavor of wild rice and adds a new twist to this pilaf.

MAKES 16 SERVINGS
(8 CUPS)

1 cup wild rice, rinsed
8 ounces snow peas or green beans, trimmed and cut diagonally into
     1$^1/_2$-inch pieces
2 cups orzo
2 large yellow bell peppers, seeded and chopped (1$^1/_2$ cups)
$^1/_2$ cup chopped red onion

DRESSING
$^2/_3$ cup cider vinegar
$^1/_2$ cup olive oil
$^1/_3$ cup chopped fresh parsley
$^1/_4$ cup peeled, grated fresh ginger root
1$^1/_2$ teaspoons Dijon mustard
Salt and freshly ground black pepper to taste

Bring a large saucepan of water to a boil. Add rice and cook until tender, about 50 minutes. Drain; transfer rice to a large mixing bowl.

Meanwhile, bring a large saucepan of water to a boil. Add snow peas or green beans and boil until bright green and just tender, about 1 minute. With a slotted spoon, scoop out beans and drain in a colander. Return water to a boil and add orzo. Cook until tender, about 10 minutes. Drain well. Add green beans, orzo, peppers and onion to rice in bowl and mix gently.

To make the dressing, in a food processor or blender, combine all ingredients and process until well blended. Pour dressing over rice mixture and toss to coat. Serve at room temperature.

Per Serving: 163 Calories; 4g Protein; 7g Fat; 21g Carbohydrates; 0mg Cholesterol; 5mg Sodium; 1g Fiber.

Would-You-Like-a-Bite Stuffed Portobello Mushroom

*Apple-Walnut Salad with Watercress and
Potato-Mushroom Soup with Apple*

Classic Onion Soup

Harvest Vegetable Pie

Layered Seitan Vegetable Dinner

Shiitake Pot Pie with Polenta Crust

Sweet Rice, Butternut Squash and Ginger

Vegetable Tagine with Olives and Prunes

Vegetarian Tourtière

Baked Stuffed Onions

Zuni Succotash

Mashed Sweet Potatoes with Parsnips and Carrots

Green Beans with Mushrooms Marsala

Apple Focaccia

Maple Syrup Baked Apples

Vegan Pumpkin Pie

Thyme-Roasted Root Vegetables

Natural sugar in root vegetables caramelizes during roasting and creates sweet-savory flavor. You can use fewer vegetables and increase more of one kind your guests prefer.

MAKES 8 SERVINGS

8 medium shallots, peeled
2 medium red-skinned potatoes, scrubbed and cut into $1\frac{1}{2}$-inch cubes
2 medium turnips, scrubbed and cut into $1\frac{1}{2}$-inch cubes
2 medium parsnips, peeled and cut into $1\frac{1}{2}$-inch cubes
4 medium carrots, scrubbed and cut into $1\frac{1}{2}$-inch slices
1 small rutabaga, peeled and cut into $1\frac{1}{2}$-inch cubes
2 cloves garlic, minced
$\frac{1}{4}$ cup olive oil
1 tablespoon chopped fresh thyme
Salt and freshly ground black pepper

Preheat oven to 450°F. In a large bowl, combine vegetables, garlic, oil, thyme, salt and pepper; toss to evenly coat. Transfer coated vegetables to a baking dish and bake until tender and browned, 35 to 40 minutes.

Per Serving: 137 Calories; 2g Protein; 7g Fat; 17g Carbohydrates; 0mg Cholesterol; 99mg Sodium; 3g Fiber.

Cranberry-Port Relish

This relish is bursting with vitamin C, is low in calories and can be made several days ahead.

MAKES 8 SERVINGS
(1½ CUPS)

1 cup fresh cranberries
$\frac{1}{4}$ cup water
$\frac{1}{2}$ cup sugar
1 tablespoon port or fresh orange juice

In a medium saucepan, combine cranberries and water. Bring to a boil, then reduce heat and simmer until cranberries are tender, 10 to 15 minutes. Stir in sugar and simmer, stirring occasionally, until sugar is dissolved. Remove from heat and stir in port or orange juice. Let cool.

Per Serving: 56 Calories; 1g Protein; 0g Fat; 14g Carbohydrates; 0mg Cholesterol; 1mg Sodium; 1g Fiber.

Baked Candied Sweet Potatoes

Candied sweet potatoes are another traditional Thanksgiving favorite. Here's a do-the-day-before version that's lighter in fat and calories and easy to reheat. Because potatoes are baked instead of boiled, flavor is not diluted with water. Besides being tasty, sweet potatoes, large edible roots, are packed with vitamins A and C.

MAKES 8 SERVINGS

8 sweet potatoes, washed but not peeled
1 teaspoon salt
2 tablespoons butter or margarine
3 tablespoons honey or maple syrup
1 teaspoon grated orange rind
$^1/_2$ teaspoon freshly ground white pepper
$^1/_4$ teaspoon mace
$^1/_2$ teaspoon cinnamon
3 tablespoons brown sugar

Pierce potatoes and bake in 400°F oven until soft, about 1 hour and 15 minutes. Remove from oven. Let rest on racks until cool enough to handle.

Cut potatoes in half. Scrape out potato flesh into a large bowl. Puree in batches in a food processor or put through a food mill. Pour puree into bowl. Add salt, butter or margarine, honey or maple syrup, orange rind, pepper and mace. Beat with an electric mixer.

Transfer to a lightly oiled ovenproof casserole. Cover top with plastic wrap lightly sprayed with vegetable oil on one side, oiled side down. Refrigerate until ready for cooking.

To heat, remove from refrigerator and bring to room temperature, about 2 hours. Preheat oven to 350°F. Remove plastic wrap from casserole. Mix cinnamon and brown sugar together with a fork, breaking up lumps. Put in a sieve; shake mixture over top of casserole. Bake until hot, about 30 minutes.

Per Serving: 187 Calories; 2g Protein; 3g Fat; 39g Carbohydrates; 8mg Cholesterol; 335mg Sodium; 3g Fiber.

Broccoli Bake

For many, a broccoli-cheese casserole topped with tons of buttered crumbs is an old-fashioned favorite. Here's a flavorful, less fat-laden version, with vegan alternatives. Besides containing vitamins A and C, this member of the cruciferous family provides riboflavin, calcium and iron.

MAKES 8 SERVINGS
(8 CUPS)

6 cups loosely packed broccoli florets
1 teaspoon salt
Water to cover
¾ cup low-fat milk or rice milk
2 tablespoons cornstarch
1 tablespoon Dijon mustard
½ teaspoon each salt and freshly ground black pepper
1 cup grated Cheddar or Cheddar-style soy cheese
½ cup soft bread crumbs
1 tablespoon olive oil
1 tablespoon freshly grated Parmesan or Parmesan-style soy cheese

Preheat oven to 350°F. Place broccoli and salt in a covered saucepan with water just to cover. Bring to rolling boil over high heat. As soon as broccoli boils, remove from pan and drain in a colander, reserving cooking liquid.

Plunge broccoli into ice water to stop cooking. Drain and set aside.

In a saucepan, place ¾ cup broccoli cooking water; add milk or rice milk. Dissolve cornstarch in a little of the liquid. Add to pan with mustard, salt and pepper. Bring to a boil, stirring constantly. Cook 3 minutes. Add Cheddar cheese or soy cheese; stir to melt.

In a bowl, combine reserved broccoli with cheese sauce. Place in a lightly oiled oven-proof casserole.

In a skillet, sauté bread crumbs with oil, stirring, until golden, about 3 minutes. In bowl, toss bread crumbs with Parmesan or Parmesan-style soy cheese to mix. Sprinkle over top of broccoli casserole. Bake until brown and bubbling, about 40 minutes.

HELPFUL HINT: *Homemade bread crumbs or bread crumbs purchased from the bakery have the best flavor and texture. Buying a 16-ounce bag of prepared ready-to-eat broccoli florets saves preparation time. One bag yields 6 cups florets.*

Per Serving: 140 Calories; 7g Protein; 8g Fat; 12g Carbohydrates; 17mg Cholesterol; 637mg Sodium; 2g Fiber.

Mashed Garlic Potatoes Champ

Champ is an old-fashioned Irish dish of scallions and mashed potatoes. Here it is enlivened with garlic and olive oil. Mashed potatoes, alas, should not be made a day ahead; however, they can be kept warm in a hot-water bath for an hour.

MAKES 8 SERVINGS
(8 CUPS)

3 pounds russet potatoes, peeled and quartered
3 garlic cloves, peeled, ends trimmed
1 1/2 teaspoons salt, divided
1/4 cup extra-virgin olive oil
1 teaspoon salt
1/2 teaspoon freshly ground white pepper
3 bunches scallions, cleaned, trimmed and chopped into 1/2-inch pieces

Place potatoes, garlic cloves and 1 teaspoon salt in a covered saucepan with water just to cover. Bring to a boil. Reduce heat; cook until potatoes are fork-tender, about 20 minutes. Drain into a colander, reserving cooking water.

While potatoes are cooking, cook scallions in a small covered saucepan in boiling water with 1/2 teaspoon salt until tender, about 5 minutes. Drain; place in ice water to stop cooking. Drain again.

In a mixer bowl, mash potatoes with a potato masher, using fork tines to mash garlic if necessary. Beat with an electric mixer, adding oil and reserved potato cooking water as needed for creamy consistency. Add remaining teaspoon salt and pepper. Stir in scallions.

Cover bowl. Set in a skillet with 2 inches simmering water to hold for serving, up to 1 hour.

Serve with butter or a small pitcher of extra-virgin olive oil if desired.

Per Serving: 212 Calories; 3g Protein; 7g Fat; 35g Carbohydrates; 0mg Cholesterol; 735mg Sodium; 3g Fiber.

Cranberry-Orange-Pecan Relish

Everyone has a favorite version of fresh cranberry relish. This one features pecans, which can be omitted.

MAKES 8 SERVINGS
(2 CUPS)

1 pound fresh cranberries, stemmed, washed and drained
2 thin-skinned oranges, washed, quartered and seeded
1½ cups sugar
1 cup finely chopped pecans

In a food processor or blender, coarsely chop cranberries in two batches; transfer to a glass or stainless-steel bowl.

In food processor or blender, coarsely chop oranges. Add orange pulp, peel and juice to cranberries. Add sugar; stir to mix. Add pecans; stir. Refrigerate, tightly covered, up to 4 days.

Per Serving: 278 Calories; 2g Protein; 9g Fat; 51g Carbohydrates; 0mg Cholesterol; 1mg Sodium; 4g Fiber.

Chou à la Bourguignonne
(Cabbage in Red Wine)

This delicious, colorful vegetable dish is perfect for a holiday table. It cooks while the family is busy with other activities.

MAKES 8 SERVINGS

$\frac{1}{2}$ tablespoon dark sesame oil
$\frac{1}{2}$ large onion, chopped
1 tart apple, peeled, cored and chopped
$1\frac{1}{2}$ pounds red cabbage, thinly shredded
$\frac{3}{4}$ cup dry red wine
$\frac{1}{2}$ cup vegetable broth
1 tablespoon red wine vinegar
$\frac{1}{2}$ bay leaf
$\frac{1}{8}$ teaspoon ground nutmeg
$\frac{1}{8}$ teaspoon ground cloves
$\frac{1}{2}$ teaspoon salt
Freshly ground black pepper to taste

Preheat oven to 325°F. In a large cast-iron skillet or flameproof casserole, heat oil over medium-high heat. Add onion; sauté 5 minutes or until soft. Add apple and cabbage; cook, stirring, until cabbage is limp. Add remaining ingredients; bring to a boil. Cover and bake 2 hours, adding water as needed. Remove bay leaf before serving.

Per Serving: 41 Calories; 1g Protein; 1g Fat; 8g Carbohydrates; 0mg Cholesterol; 155mg Sodium; 2g Fiber.

Glazed Shallots and Walnuts

This is an interesting combination made unique with a touch of cinnamon.

$1\frac{1}{2}$ pounds shallots, trimmed and peeled
$1\frac{1}{2}$ cups water
2 tablespoons butter or margarine
2 tablespoons sugar
$\frac{1}{4}$ teaspoon cinnamon
$\frac{1}{2}$ teaspoon salt
2 cups walnut halves

If shallots are large, cut into halves or quarters. Place all ingredients except walnuts in a wide skillet; bring to a boil. Reduce heat, cover and simmer 5 minutes. Remove lid and cook an additional 10 minutes, turning shallots occasionally. Add walnuts and cook until very little liquid remains, about 5 minutes.

Spoon remaining liquid over shallots and walnuts to glaze before serving.

Per Serving: 293 Calories; 7g Protein; 22g Fat; 23g Carbohydrates; 8mg Cholesterol; 190mg Sodium; 2g Fiber.

Orange-Glazed Snow Peas

A citrusy orange glaze is made richer with the addition of cloves and cardamom.

Makes 6 servings

$\frac{1}{2}$ cup fresh orange juice
2 tablespoons julienned orange zest
2 tablespoons honey
1 tablespoon butter or margarine
$\frac{1}{8}$ teaspoon ground cardamom
Dash ground cloves (optional)
$1\frac{1}{4}$ pounds snow peas

Combine all ingredients except snow peas in a small saucepan; simmer until reduced to about ¼ cup. Blanch snow peas in boiling water about 30 seconds; drain. Immediately transfer snow peas to serving dish. Pour orange sauce over snow peas and toss to coat. Serve hot.

🍂 Per Serving: 90 Calories; 3g Protein; 2g Fat; 15g Carbohydrates; 6mg Cholesterol; 245mg Sodium; 3g Fiber.

Corn Sautéed with Mint and Shiitake Mushrooms

This side dish is flavorful, a bit exotic and quick to prepare.

MAKES 6 SERVINGS

8 ounces shiitake or other wild mushrooms
2 tablespoons butter or margarine
Kernels from 6 ears fresh corn or 16-ounce bag frozen corn
3 tablespoons chopped fresh mint
$^1/_2$ teaspoon salt
Freshly ground pepper to taste

Remove mushroom stems. Slice mushrooms; sauté in butter or margarine over medium heat about 2 minutes, or until limp. Add corn, mint, salt and pepper; cook 3 more minutes, stirring. Serve immediately.

🍂 Per Serving: 105 Calories; 3g Protein; 2g Fat; 23g Carbohydrates; 4mg Cholesterol; 213mg Sodium; 1g Fiber.

Baked Stuffed Onions

This hearty side dish stands up well to reheating.

MAKES 4 SERVINGS

4 medium yellow onions, peeled
2 tablespoons honey or other sweetener
$\frac{1}{2}$ cup finely chopped walnuts
$\frac{1}{2}$ cup wheat germ or bread crumbs
$\frac{1}{2}$ teaspoon salt
$\frac{1}{4}$ teaspoon freshly ground black pepper
2 teaspoons Dijon mustard
1 tablespoon red wine vinegar
$\frac{1}{4}$ cup chopped fresh Italian parsley for garnish

Preheat oven to 350°F. Slice about $\frac{1}{2}$ inch off top of each onion. With a melon baller, hollow out a bowl-shaped space in top of each onion to hold about $\frac{1}{4}$ cup filling. Slice off enough of bottom of each onion to stand upright.

In a medium bowl, combine all remaining ingredients except parsley. Place onions in a baking dish. Pour about $\frac{1}{3}$ cup water around onions; bake 30 minutes. (Add water about $\frac{1}{4}$ cup at a time if it evaporates during baking.)

Remove onions from oven; spoon filling into onions and over tops. Return to oven and bake until softened, about 30 minutes. Garnish with parsley. Serve warm.

Per Serving: 213 Calories; 8g Protein; 11g Fat; 25g Carbohydrates; 0mg Cholesterol; 312mg Sodium; 4g Fiber.

Honey-Glazed Onions

A nest of confetti-colored vegetables and a honey-mustard glaze elevate a simple onion to a lovely holiday dish. These can be made ahead and reheated just before serving time, and are good for a crowd.

MAKES 20 SERVINGS

FILLING

10 medium onions (a sweet variety)
1 cup seasoned bread crumbs
1 cup corn kernels, frozen or canned
1 cup diced zucchini
1 cup grated carrots
1 cup diced canned beets
1 cup water

GLAZE

$\frac{1}{2}$ cup honey
3 tablespoons Dijon mustard
2 tablespoons balsamic or red wine vinegar
2 teaspoons paprika
$\frac{1}{2}$ teaspoon ground ginger
$1\frac{1}{2}$ teaspoons salt, plus more to taste
1 teaspoon freshly ground black pepper, plus more to taste

Preheat oven to 350°F. Peel onions; slice in half on the equator. Remove centers, leaving a "bowl" in center of onion halves.

To prepare the filling, in a bowl, stir together ½ cup bread crumbs and all the corn, zucchini, carrots and beets. Firmly pack, filling in hollowed-out onion halves, and arrange in a shallow baking dish so that onions fit snugly. Pour water around base of onions.

To make the glaze, in a separate bowl, whisk together glaze ingredients. Drizzle half of mixture over tops of stuffed onions. Bake 30 minutes. Drizzle with remaining glaze sauce. Bake 30 minutes more.

Just before serving, sprinkle onions with remaining ½ cup bread crumbs and place onions under broiler until crumbs are toasted and golden brown.

🍃 Per Serving: 67 Calories; 2g Protein; 1g Fat; 15g Carbohydrates; 0mg Cholesterol; 272mg Sodium; 1g Fiber.

Fluffy Mashed Sweet Potatoes

This dish is part of the meal but is sweet enough for dessert.

MAKES 6 SERVINGS

2 cups cooked and mashed sweet potatoes (2 small or 1 large sweet potato)
3 bananas, mashed
1½ cups soymilk or milk
½ cup prune juice
3 tablespoons honey
1 teaspoon allspice
2 teaspoons chopped candied ginger

Preheat oven to 375°F. Combine all ingredients except ginger and beat until fluffy. Pour into an oiled casserole and bake 50 to 60 minutes, until golden brown. Sprinkle with candied ginger.

Per Serving: 277 Calories; 5g Protein; 1g Fat; 64g Carbohydrates; 0mg Cholesterol; 31mg Sodium; 6g Fiber.

Zuni Succotash

The word *succotash* comes from a Narragansett Indian word meaning "boiled whole kernels of corn." The heat in this version can be adjusted, depending on the type of chilies used.

MAKES 8 SERVINGS

6 cobs fresh corn
¼ cup butter, margarine or vegetable oil
1 cup finely diced onion
2 cups cooked beans, such as red, pinto, adzuki or cranberry
2 poblano chilies, roasted, peeled and finely diced
1 medium zucchini, finely diced
1 cup water
Salt and freshly ground black pepper to taste

Cut corn kernels off cobs. Heat butter, margarine or oil; sauté onion over low heat until translucent. Add corn. Cook 5 minutes over low heat, stirring constantly.

Add beans, chilies and zucchini; stir well. Add water; cook over low heat 15 minutes, stirring every 3 minutes. (Corn will caramelize slightly.) Season with salt and pepper.

Per Serving: 183 Calories; 6g Protein; 7g Fat; 27g Carbohydrates; 16mg Cholesterol; 92mg Sodium; 6g Fiber.

Wild Rice with Dried Fruit

Wild rice is expensive but has a wonderful crunchy texture and nutty flavor. If you wish, cook 1 cup of wild rice and 1 cup of brown rice separately, then combine them with the fruit and nuts.

Makes 8 servings

    2 cups long-grain wild rice
    $\frac{1}{2}$ cup pitted prunes
    $\frac{1}{2}$ cup dried cherries or cranberries
    1 cup chopped pecans
    $\frac{1}{2}$ cup water
    Salt to taste

Cook rice according to package directions, or until ends break open like flowers, about 1 hour; drain.

Cut each prune in 8 pieces; add to rice with cherries or cranberries and pecans. Add $\frac{1}{2}$ cup water and salt. Cover pan; cook mixture over low heat or in 300°F oven 15 minutes. Stir before serving.

Per Serving: 308 Calories; 5g Protein; 10g Fat; 50g Carbohydrates; 0mg Cholesterol; 5mg Sodium; 2g Fiber.

String Beans with Julienned Vegetables

This dish makes a beautiful presentation. Julienned vegetables are often used as garnish for dishes. Here they feature prominently in the dish itself.

Makes 4 servings

$\frac{1}{3}$ cup olive oil or other vegetable oil
$\frac{1}{4}$ cup rice vinegar
2 tablespoons fresh tarragon (1 tablespoon dried)
1 tablespoon Dijon mustard
1 teaspoon sugar
$\frac{1}{2}$ teaspoon salt
$\frac{1}{2}$ teaspoon freshly ground black pepper
$\frac{1}{2}$ pound string beans, halved, blanched and without stems
1 small to medium red onion, slivered
1 red or yellow bell pepper, cut into strips
$\frac{1}{2}$ pound jícama, peeled and julienned, or 1 large carrot, julienned
1 jalapeño pepper, seeded and minced (optional)
$\frac{1}{2}$ cup slivered almonds

In a medium bowl, whisk together oil, vinegar, tarragon, mustard, sugar, salt and pepper. Add beans, onion, bell pepper, jícama or carrot, jalapeño if desired and almonds; toss thoroughly. Chill 1 hour. Serve over a bed of lettuce.

Per Serving: 307 Calories; 6g Protein; 27g Fat; 12g Carbohydrates; 0mg Cholesterol; 395mg Sodium; 4g Fiber.

Mashed Sweet Potatoes with Parsnips and Carrots

Sweet potatoes are high in beta carotene, vitamin C and fiber and always make an appearance at the Thanksgiving meal. Here's a new way to prepare them.

MAKES 6 SERVINGS

2 medium sweet potatoes, peeled and cut into 1-inch cubes
2 large carrots, peeled and cut into 1-inch cubes
2 large parsnips, peeled and cut into 1-inch chunks
Water to cover
1 teaspoon cinnamon
1 teaspoon freshly grated nutmeg
Pinch salt
1/4 cup melted margarine or butter
1/4 cup warm skim milk, soymilk or other nondairy milk

In a large saucepan or Dutch oven over high heat, add sweet potatoes, carrots, parsnips and water to cover. Reduce heat and simmer until tender, about 15 to 20 minutes. Drain. Transfer to a large bowl.

With a potato ricer or potato masher, mash vegetables. Add cinnamon, nutmeg and salt. Alternately add margarine or butter and milk; whip until fluffy.

Per Serving: 175 Calories; 2g Protein; 8g Fat; 25g Carbohydrates; 0mg Cholesterol; 126mg Sodium; 5g Fiber.

Sweet Potato, Carrots and Spiced Fruits

This earthy, colorful dish is simple to prepare and has a creative combination of flavors and textures.

Makes 6 servings

2 medium sweet potatoes, peeled and cut into 1-inch cubes
2 large carrots, peeled and cut into 1-inch cubes
6 dried peaches or apricots
6 dried, pitted prunes
$\frac{1}{4}$ cup golden raisins
1 teaspoon curry powder
1 teaspoon cinnamon
1 teaspoon coriander
$1\frac{1}{2}$ cups apple juice
1 large unpeeled Bosc pear, cut into 1-inch cubes
$\frac{1}{4}$ cup cranberries

In a large saucepan or Dutch oven, add all ingredients except pear and cranberries. Cook over medium heat until sweet potatoes and carrots are crisp-tender, about 15 minutes. Increase heat to medium-high; cook until liquid is reduced by half.

Add pear and cranberries; cook until cranberries pop, about 5 minutes. Serve at room temperature.

🍂 Per Serving: 206 Calories; 3g Protein; 1g Fat; 52g Carbohydrates; 0mg Cholesterol; 17mg Sodium; 8g Fiber.

Cinnamon-Glazed Carrots

This side dish is a must at holiday dinners.

MAKES 6 SERVINGS

1 pound carrots, peeled and sliced into $1/4$-inch-thick rounds (about $3\frac{1}{2}$ cups)
$1/3$ cup unsweetened apple juice concentrate, thawed
$1/2$ teaspoon ground cinnamon

Combine ingredients in a large saucepan and stir well. Bring to a simmer, cover and cook over moderate heat for 15 to 20 minutes, until carrots are tender-crisp. Cook uncovered 3 to 5 minutes more, or until liquid is reduced to a glaze.

HELPFUL HINT: *With a long, sharp knife, you can slice three carrots placed side-by-side at the same time.*

Per Serving: 60 Calories; 1g Protein; 0g Fat; 14g Carbohydrates; 0mg Cholesterol; 30mg Sodium; 3g Fiber.

Green Beans with Mushrooms Marsala

Here's a really easy green bean dish. The Marsala gives it a rich taste, just right for a holiday dinner.

MAKES 6 SERVINGS

1 pound green beans, ends trimmed
1 tablespoon extra-virgin olive oil
1 clove minced garlic
1 pound white or brown mushrooms, trimmed and sliced $\frac{1}{8}$ inch thick
1 teaspoon salt
$\frac{1}{2}$ teaspoon freshly ground black pepper
$\frac{1}{4}$ cup sweet Marsala wine or sherry

Lay green beans in steamer of choice; cover. Steam over high heat until beans are crisp-tender, about 15 minutes.

While beans are steaming, heat oil over high heat in a large nonstick skillet. Add garlic; cook, stirring, until garlic is cooked through but not brown. Add mushrooms; cook, stirring and flipping, until mushrooms exude moisture and begin to brown, about 7 minutes. Add seasonings and wine or sherry; stir. Continue cooking until alcohol evaporates, 1 to 2 minutes. Cover with lid; set aside.

When beans are steamed, transfer to a serving plate. Pour mushrooms over top. Serve immediately.

VARIATIONS: *Serve steamed green beans drizzled with a mixture of fresh lemon juice and extra-virgin olive oil. Add salt and black pepper to taste. Or chill steamed green beans, then toss in a vinaigrette and serve on a bed of crisp lettuces.*

Per Serving: 80 Calories; 3g Protein; 3g Fat; 11g Carbohydrates; 0mg Cholesterol; 393mg Sodium; 4g Fiber.

Sweet Potato and Parsnip Casserole

This casserole benefits from a day in the refrigerator to give its flavors time to meld, making it a nice do-ahead Thanksgiving side dish.

MAKES 8 SERVINGS

1½ tablespoons olive oil, plus 1 teaspoon for drizzling
3 large onions, thinly sliced (about 4 cups)
5 cloves garlic, minced
3 to 4 large sweet potatoes (about 2 pounds), peeled and cut into
    ¼-inch slices
1 pound parsnips, peeled and cut into ¼-inch slices
2 to 3 cups Basic Vegetable Stock (recipe follows)
1 cup nonfat sour cream
1 teaspoon fresh or dried thyme
Salt and freshly ground black pepper
¼ cup bread crumbs

Preheat oven to 400°F. Heat 1½ tablespoons oil in a large nonstick skillet. Add onions and garlic; cook over medium heat until deep golden brown, about 10 to 15 minutes, stirring often.

Stir in sweet potatoes and parsnips. Add stock, sour cream, thyme and a little salt and pepper. Simmer until potatoes are tender and most of liquid is absorbed, 15 to 20 minutes. Add more salt and pepper to taste. Transfer to a 2-quart baking dish. (Mixture can be refrigerated at this point and baked later.)

Sprinkle casserole with bread crumbs and drizzle with remaining 1 teaspoon olive oil. Bake casserole until stock has been absorbed and top browns, about 20 minutes. (Or brown casserole under broiler if stock is absorbed before casserole browns.)

Per Serving: 186 Calories; 5g Protein; 5g Fat; 32g Carbohydrates; 0mg Cholesterol; 315mg Sodium; 4g Fiber.

Basic Vegetable Stock

Here's an all-purpose stock that's tasty and easy to prepare.

MAKES ABOUT 3 QUARTS
(12 CUPS)

1 large onion (with skin), quartered
2 leeks, cut into 1-inch pieces
2 carrots, cut into 1-inch pieces
2 stalks celery, cut into 1-inch pieces
2 tomatoes, roughly chopped
1 head garlic (with peel), cut in half
2 quarts chopped vegetables or vegetable trimmings (see Hint)
2 tablespoons tomato paste
Bouquet garni (see Hint)
½ cup chopped fresh herbs, including basil, oregano, chives and/or
    parsley stems
4 quarts water
Freshly ground black pepper
Salt or soy sauce to taste

Combine all ingredients except pepper and salt or soy sauce in a large pot; bring to a boil. Skim off foam that has risen to top. Immediately lower heat and simmer, uncovered, until well flavored, 1 to 2 hours. Add water as necessary to keep vegetables covered. Skim as necessary. Season to taste with pepper and salt or soy sauce at end of cooking time.

Strain stock, pressing vegetables with back of spoon to extract as much liquid as possible. For a thicker stock, puree vegetables in a food mill or blender, add to liquid and strain. Cool stock to room temperature, then refrigerate or freeze.

HELPFUL HINTS:

- *Onions, carrots, celery, leeks, garlic, tomatoes, corn cobs and husks, summer and winter squash, parsnips, turnips, mushrooms, green beans, potatoes, eggplant, bell peppers, kale, collard greens and cabbage are all good options to be chopped up for use in stock.*

- *To make bouquet garni, tie together sprigs of parsley, thyme and bay leaf or place in a cheesecloth bag. Alternatively, wrap herbs in aluminum foil and pierce foil with a fork.*

VARIATION: *For a richer, more flavorful vegetable stock, roast vegetables in a lightly oiled roasting pan in a 400°F oven until browned, about 45 minutes. (You may oil the vegetables lightly with olive oil to keep them from drying out.) Transfer vegetables to a stockpot. Deglaze roasting pan with ½ cup dry white wine and add to stockpot as well. Continue with recipe.*

🌿 Per Cup: 318 Calories; 9g Protein; 2g Fat; 73g Carbohydrates; 0mg Cholesterol; 140mg Sodium; 13g Fiber.

Carrots on Carrots

These carrots taste good hot, cold or at room temperature. They can be presented on their own, in a salad with peppers and cucumbers or as an ingredient in pasta primavera.

MAKES 2 SERVINGS

2 teaspoons olive oil
½ teaspoon dried rosemary or thyme, or a mixture
½ pound carrots (4 medium), scraped and sliced into ¼-inch rounds
1 cup fresh carrot juice
1 to 2 tablespoons white wine vinegar
½ teaspoon salt, or to taste
¼ cup chopped fresh mint or flat-leaf parsley, or a mixture

Heat oil with dried herbs in a small saucepan. Add carrots, stirring to coat with oil-and-herb mixture. Add carrot juice, vinegar and salt. Bring to a boil. Lower heat and cook slowly, uncovered, until carrots are tender, about 20 minutes, adding a small amount of water if necessary to prevent sticking. (Just enough liquid should be left in pan to lightly coat the carrots.) Remove from heat; stir in mint or parsley.

🌿 Per Serving: 155 Calories; 3g Protein; 5g Fat; 27g Carbohydrates; 0mg Cholesterol; 623mg Sodium; 6g Fiber.

Paprika Mashed Potatoes

This version of mashed potatoes offers old-fashioned flavor with more color and less fat than traditional recipes. Vary the flavor by adding ½ tablespoon of any dried herb.

MAKES 6 SERVINGS

6 medium-sized baking potatoes, peeled and diced
¾ cup plain nonfat yogurt
¼ cup evaporated skim milk or low-fat soymilk
½ tablespoon paprika
Salt to taste
½ teaspoon freshly ground black pepper
1 teaspoon melted unsalted butter or soy margarine

Place potatoes in a saucepan, add cold water to cover and bring to a boil. Reduce heat, partially cover and gently boil about 20 minutes or until tender. Drain. Combine potatoes with yogurt, milk or soymilk, paprika, salt and pepper. Mash or beat with an electric mixer until smooth. Drizzle with butter or soy margarine.

Per Serving: 152 Calories; 5g Protein; 1g Fat; 32g Carbohydrates; 2mg Cholesterol; 42mg Sodium; 3g Fiber.

Braised Leeks and Mushrooms

Wild mushrooms lend a distinct flavor to this dish. If using shiitake mushrooms, take care to use only the caps. The stems are usually tough; reserve them to make stock.

MAKES 6 SERVINGS

$^1/_4$ cup dry sherry
1 teaspoon olive oil
5 cups thinly sliced leeks (see Hint)
1 cup thinly sliced fresh wild mushrooms, such as chanterelle or shiitake caps
1 teaspoon fresh orange juice
$^1/_2$ teaspoon grated orange peel
1 tablespoon apple cider vinegar
Salt or herbal salt substitute and freshly ground black pepper to taste

In a large skillet over medium-high heat, combine sherry and oil. Heat to simmering, then add leeks. Sauté, stirring frequently, 3 minutes. Add mushrooms and sauté 5 minutes, or until mushrooms exude moisture. Stir in orange juice, orange peel and vinegar. Remove from heat. Add seasonings and serve warm.

HELPFUL HINT: *To prepare leeks, slice in half lengthwise. Wash well, making sure to remove the dirt that often is lodged between layers.*

 Per Serving: 24 Calories; 0g Protein; 1g Fat; 2g Carbohydrates; 0mg Cholesterol; 1mg Sodium; 0g Fiber.

Hartzie's Cranberry Mold

Early preparation is no problem with this dish. You can make this recipe up to 3 days ahead.

MAKES 6 SERVINGS

2 cups fresh cranberries
4 large juice oranges, peeled and juiced (separate and retain pulp)
2 tablespoons maple syrup
1/2 cup agar flakes

In a food processor or grinder, grind cranberries and orange pulp until coarse. Set aside. Combine orange juice, maple syrup and agar flakes in a saucepan over medium-high heat and bring to a boil. Simmer, stirring, until agar flakes dissolve. (Make sure flakes completely dissolve; otherwise the dish will not gel properly.) Combine with cranberry mixture and stir well. Spoon into a decorative mold or casserole and refrigerate until firm. When set, rinse outside of container under hot water and turn mold onto a platter to serve.

Per Serving: 82 Calories; 1g Protein; 0g Fat; 21g Carbohydrates; 0mg Cholesterol; 3mg Sodium; 4g Fiber.

Baked Sweet Potatoes and Red Potatoes

This recipe has the perfect balance of sweet and savory.

MAKES 6 SERVINGS

3 large sweet potatoes, unpeeled, cut into 1/2-inch-thick slices
8 small red potatoes, unpeeled, halved
1 tablespoon olive oil
Freshly ground black pepper

Preheat oven to 400°F. Place sweet potatoes and red potatoes on an ungreased baking sheet. Lightly brush tops with oil and sprinkle with pepper. Bake 30 to 40 minutes, or until soft and lightly browned. Place in a serving dish.

Per Serving: 225 Calories; 4g Protein; 2g Fat; 48g Carbohydrates; 0mg Cholesterol; 17mg Sodium; 5g Fiber.

Bulgur-Almond Stuffing

Here's a light, crunchy stuffing made of bulgur, apples and nuts. Almonds, hazelnuts, pecans, pine nuts and walnuts are all equally delicious.

MAKES 6 SERVINGS

1$^1/_2$ cups bulgur
2$^1/_2$ cups boiling water
$^1/_2$ to 1 cup sliced almonds or other nuts
1 bunch (about 8) scallions, sliced thinly
1 Rome or Cortland apple, chopped
$^1/_4$ teaspoon dried thyme
$^1/_2$ teaspoon salt
$^1/_4$ teaspoon freshly ground black pepper
2 to 3 tablespoons soy margarine or butter

Place bulgur in a medium bowl. Pour in water, cover and let sit for 1 hour.

Preheat oven to 350°F. Add to bulgur the nuts, scallions, apple, thyme, salt and pepper; toss well. Transfer mixture to a medium baking dish. Cut margarine or butter into small pieces and place on bulgur. Bake 15 minutes. Serve hot or warm.

🍂 Per Serving: 233 Calories; 7g Protein; 10g Fat; 32g Carbohydrates; 0mg Cholesterol; 201mg Sodium; 8g Fiber.

Wild Rice and Apricot Stuffing

Here's an all-time, year-round favorite.

Makes 8 servings

1 cup wild rice
3 cups water
$\frac{1}{2}$ teaspoon salt
2 to 4 tablespoons soy margarine or butter
2 shallots, minced
1 garlic clove, minced
1 cup dried apricots, chopped
$\frac{1}{4}$ cup chopped fresh parsley
$\frac{1}{4}$ teaspoon freshly ground black pepper

Cook rice with water and ¼ teaspoon salt in a medium saucepan, covered, for 60 minutes or until grains split open. Drain any excess water and allow rice to cool.

Melt margarine or butter in a small skillet; add shallots and garlic, and sauté 2 minutes. In a medium bowl, combine sautéed vegetables with rice, apricots, parsley, pepper and remaining ¼ teaspoon salt.

Preheat oven to 350°F. Transfer rice mixture to a medium baking dish, cover and bake 15 minutes. Serve hot or at room temperature.

Per Serving: 149 Calories; 4g Protein; 3g Fat; 28g Carbohydrates; 0mg Cholesterol; 150mg Sodium; 1g Fiber.

Stuffed Thanksgiving Pumpkins

Look for miniature pumpkins at the supermarket from late October through December. Hollowed out, they make charming tureens for individual servings of soup or this delicious herb and vegetable stuffing.

MAKES 8 SERVINGS

8 baby pumpkins
$1/3$ cup vegetable stock or water
$1/2$ cup finely chopped onion
2 large cloves garlic, minced
$1/2$ teaspoon dried sage leaves
$1/2$ teaspoon dried thyme
1 cup whole-wheat bread crumbs
$1/4$ cup toasted pine nuts (optional)
$1/3$ cup finely chopped celery
$1/4$ cup chopped dried apricots
$1/2$ cup grated part-skim mozzarella cheese (optional)
Low-sodium soy sauce or salt to taste

Preheat oven to 350°F. Slice off the top $1/2$ inch of each pumpkin and scoop out the seeds. Bake pumpkins for 15 minutes.

In a large skillet over medium-high heat, heat stock or water to simmering and add onion. Stir well and cook, stirring frequently, 8 minutes, or until onions are softened but not browned. Add garlic, sage, thyme and bread crumbs. Cook, stirring, 1 minute, then remove from heat and stir in remaining ingredients. Lightly fill pumpkins with stuffing. (Any remaining stuffing may be baked separately in a lightly oiled baking dish.)

Bake 15 minutes, or until stuffing is lightly browned and heated through. Be careful not to overbake pumpkins, because they will split.

Per Serving: 152 Calories; 6g Protein; 4g Fat; 28g Carbohydrates; 0mg Cholesterol; 249mg Sodium; 5g Fiber.

Spinach with Pine Nuts and Raisins

This dish combines sweet and savory flavors. Serve it as you would any vegetable side dish.

3 pounds fresh spinach, cleaned and trimmed
2 tablespoons olive oil
2 cloves garlic, minced
$^1/_3$ cup pine nuts, toasted
$^1/_2$ cup raisins, coarsely chopped
$^1/_2$ teaspoon salt
$^1/_4$ teaspoon freshly ground black pepper

Bring a large pot of water to a boil. Blanch spinach by dropping in water for 45 seconds. Drain spinach; chop and set aside.

In a heavy skillet, heat oil. Add spinach and remaining ingredients. Cook over medium heat 10 minutes, stirring frequently, until spinach has wilted. Serve hot or at room temperature.

HELPFUL HINT: *If you don't have fresh spinach, use two 10-ounce packages of frozen chopped spinach, thawed and squeezed dry. Add directly to skillet with remaining ingredients.*

 Per Serving: 259 Calories; 14g Protein; 15g Fat; 29g Carbohydrates; 0mg Cholesterol; 562mg Sodium; 11g Fiber.

Ginger Applesauce

Fresh ginger root and lemon zest give this applesauce a special zing.

10 Cortland apples
1 cup apple cider
2 cinnamon sticks
1½ teaspoons lemon zest
¼ cup light brown sugar
¼ teaspoon ground nutmeg
1½ tablespoons finely chopped ginger root

Peel, core and chop apples. Transfer to a large saucepan and add cider, cinnamon and lemon zest. Simmer over medium heat 30 minutes, stirring occasionally. Remove cinnamon sticks. Add sugar, nutmeg and ginger, and cook until thick, about 10 minutes. Serve warm or chilled.

Per Serving: 118 Calories; 0g Protein; 1g Fat; 31g Carbohydrates; 0mg Cholesterol; 4mg Sodium; 5g Fiber.

Baked Sweet Potatoes with Yogurt-Rice Topping

The tart topping balances the sweetness of the potatoes in this simple low-fat dish. This is best served warm but is good at any temperature.

MAKES 6 SERVINGS

6 small sweet potatoes
¾ cup plain nonfat yogurt
½ cup warm cooked rice
Salt and freshly ground white pepper to taste

Preheat oven to 450°F. Score the surface of sweet potatoes with a fork several times and bake 35 to 40 minutes, or until tender. Slit each one down the middle and remove a couple of tablespoons flesh to make room for filling. Reserve flesh for another use. Wrap potatoes in foil and set aside.

In a separate bowl, combine yogurt and rice. Add salt and pepper. Refrigerate until ready to serve.

Place potatoes on a serving dish. Fold back foil to make a "boat" and spoon on topping.

VARIATION: *Replace some of the rice with wild rice, add chopped herbs and dried apricots and garnish with toasted pecans.*

Per Serving: 151 Calories; 4g Protein; 0g Fat; 34g Carbohydrates; 0mg Cholesterol; 36mg Sodium; 3g Fiber.

Mashed Celery Root and Potatoes

What's Thanksgiving without the soothing, comforting taste of creamy mashed potatoes? Celery root (also called "celeriac") adds a definite celery taste but with a smooth, rich texture.

MAKES 8 SERVINGS

1 pound celery root, peeled and cut into 2-inch cubes (about 3 cups)
1 pound all-purpose potatoes, peeled and cut into 2-inch cubes (about 2 cups)
2 tablespoons butter or margarine
2 tablespoons sour or heavy cream
Salt and freshly ground black pepper to taste
1 tablespoon chopped fresh chives

Place celery root and potatoes in a large saucepan, cover with cold water and bring to a boil. Boil, partially covered, until tender, about 15 minutes. Drain, reserving about 1 cup of cooking liquid. Mash vegetables thoroughly with a potato masher. Add butter or margarine, cream and enough reserved cooking liquid (about ¾ cup) to make a light and creamy consistency. Season with salt and pepper. Transfer to a warmed serving dish and sprinkle with the chopped chives.

Per Serving: 82 Calories; 1g Protein; 5g Fat; 9g Carbohydrates; 10mg Cholesterol; 239mg Sodium; 1g Fiber.

Sweet Potato Stuffing

This flavorful stuffing goes well with any gravy, but Chunky Tomato Gravy (page 151) is a sure bet.

Makes 8 servings

1$\frac{1}{2}$ pounds sweet potatoes, peeled and cut into chunks (about 6 cups)
Water for cooking
3 to 4 tablespoons butter or soy margarine
1 bunch (about 8) scallions, chopped finely
2 eggs (or 1 tablespoon Egg Replacer and $\frac{1}{4}$ cup water)
1 cup plus 2 tablespoons fresh whole-wheat bread crumbs
$\frac{1}{4}$ teaspoon freshly ground black pepper
$\frac{1}{2}$ teaspoon salt
$\frac{1}{2}$ teaspoon orange zest
3 tablespoons chopped fresh parsley

Place sweet potatoes in a medium saucepan with enough water to cover. Cook over medium-high heat until tender, about 25 minutes. Drain off water. Transfer potatoes to a food processor or blender and puree with 1 tablespoon butter or margarine.

Meanwhile, sauté scallions in 1 to 2 tablespoons butter or margarine for 1 minute. In a medium bowl, combine pureed potatoes, sautéed scallions, eggs (or Egg Replacer), 1 cup bread crumbs, pepper, salt, zest and parsley. Mix well and set aside.

In a small skillet, melt remaining 1 tablespoon butter or margarine. Add remaining 2 tablespoons bread crumbs and toast over medium-high heat.

Preheat oven to 350°F. Spoon stuffing mixture into an oval gratin dish or baking dish. Sprinkle toasted bread crumbs over stuffing and bake 20 minutes, or until set. Serve hot.

Per Serving: 200 Calories; 5g Protein; 7g Fat; 30g Carbohydrates; 65mg Cholesterol; 769mg Sodium; 3g Fiber.

GREAT GRAVIES
and Table Sauces

*I*f the term "comfort food" appeared in the dictionary, "gravy" would have to be listed as part of the definition. Whether poured on the side, drizzled over the top or smothered and swabbed with a hunk of bread, down-home gravy lends soothing, straight-from-the-hearth flavors and textures to the main course. Like a familiar face in a crowd, a gravy boat is a reassuring sight on the holiday table. Gravy will surely appear on everyone's quintessential Thanksgiving menu.

As this chapter aptly illustrates, a plethora of meat-free gravies come to life in the vegetarian kitchen. Inventive recipes such as Mushroom-Walnut Gravy, Chunky Tomato Gravy, simple Brown Gravy and other enticing table sauces offer vivid proof that not all gravies are born in a roasting pan. These tempting gravies can enhance a variety of grain, rice and vegetable dishes, and most important, promise to make a memorable contribution to your meatless Thanksgiving feast.

Like soups and chowders, most gravy recipes can be prepared ahead of time, refrigerated and gradually reheated in a saucepan just before dinner. As a rule, plan to make more gravy than you think you'll ever need. If you have a little extra gravy resting on the stovetop, you won't fret when ol' Uncle Buck absent-mindedly dumps half of the gravy boat onto his plate before passing it on to the rest of the table.

Chunky Tomato Gravy

This pretty, bright-red gravy goes well with any stuffing. It may not be traditional, but who's to quibble?

MAKES 4 SERVINGS

2 tablespoons soy margarine or butter
1 onion, minced
1 garlic clove, minced
$\frac{1}{2}$ pound plum tomatoes (about 3), peeled, seeded and chopped
2 teaspoons arrowroot powder or cornstarch
$\frac{1}{4}$ teaspoon salt
$\frac{1}{8}$ teaspoon freshly ground black pepper
1 cup water
$\frac{1}{4}$ cup chopped fresh parsley

Melt margarine or butter in a medium saucepan; add onion and garlic, and sauté over medium-high heat about 1 minute. Add tomatoes and cook another 2 minutes. Stir in arrowroot or cornstarch, salt, pepper and water. Cook, stirring, until thickened, about 4 to 5 minutes. Stir in parsley. Transfer to a serving dish and serve hot.

Per Serving: 55 Calories; 1g Protein; 2g Fat; 8g Carbohydrates; 5mg Cholesterol; 175mg Sodium; 2g Fiber.

Mushroom Gravy

This delicious, rich-tasting gravy has a velvety texture. It is particularly good with Wild Rice and Apricot Stuffing (see recipe, page 141).

Makes 5 servings

2½ tablespoons soy margarine or butter
½ pound mushrooms, sliced ¼ inch thick (about 2⅓ cups)
3 tablespoons all-purpose flour
2 cups vegetable broth
¼ teaspoon dried thyme
¼ teaspoon salt
⅛ teaspoon freshly ground black pepper

Melt 1 tablespoon margarine or butter in a medium skillet. Add mushrooms and cook over medium heat 3 minutes. Remove mushrooms with a slotted spoon and set aside.

Add remaining 1½ tablespoons margarine or butter and flour to skillet; whisk until smooth and cook 30 seconds. Add broth slowly while continuing to whisk. Cook 1 minute, then stir in reserved mushrooms, thyme, salt and pepper. Cook, stirring, about 2 minutes more. Pour into a serving dish.

Per Serving: 50 Calories; 2g Protein; 3g Fat; 6g Carbohydrates; 5mg Cholesterol; 538 Mg Sodium; 1g Fiber.

Brown Gravy

Try this gravy with Bulgur-Almond Stuffing (page 140) or Sweet Potato Stuffing (page 147).

MAKES 5 SERVINGS

2$\frac{1}{2}$ tablespoons soy margarine or butter
$\frac{1}{4}$ cup all-purpose flour
1$\frac{1}{2}$ cups vegetable broth
2 tablespoons soy sauce
$\frac{1}{4}$ teaspoon freshly ground black pepper
$\frac{1}{4}$ cup chopped fresh parsley

Melt margarine or butter in a small saucepan over medium heat. Add flour and whisk together about 30 seconds; then add broth slowly while whisking. Cook over medium heat for 2 minutes. Add soy sauce and pepper. Continue cooking until gravy achieves desired thickness. Transfer to a gravy boat or dish and stir in parsley. Serve warm.

 Per Serving: 49 Calories; 2g Protein; 2g Fat; 6g Carbohydrates; 5mg Cholesterol; 732mg Sodium; 0g Fiber.

Rich Mushroom Sauce

This easy sauce makes a luscious topping for the Golden Lentil Roulade with Chestnut Stuffing (page 73) and the savory Mashed Celery Root and Potatoes (page 146).

MAKES 16 SERVINGS
(3 CUPS)

2 tablespoons olive oil
1 medium onion, chopped
2 cloves garlic, minced
1½ cups cremini mushrooms, chopped
2¼ cups water
3 tablespoons soy sauce
1 teaspoon vegetable bouillon powder
2 teaspoons cornstarch dissolved in ¼ cup water
Salt and freshly ground black pepper to taste

In a medium saucepan, heat oil over medium heat. Add onion and garlic and cook, stirring often, until onion is soft, about 5 minutes. Add mushrooms and cook, stirring often, until they begin to release their juices. Add water, soy sauce, bouillon powder and dissolved cornstarch; stir well. Simmer until thickened slightly, about 10 minutes. Season with salt and pepper.

 Per Serving: 25 Calories; 0g Protein; 2g Fat; 2g Carbohydrates; 0mg Cholesterol; 257mg Sodium; 0g Fiber.

Mushroom-Walnut Gravy

This gravy gets its flavor from dried mushrooms and browned flour. But burned flour is bitter, so cook carefully. Brown flour has half the thickening capacity of white flour, so this recipe calls for 8 tablespoons, just enough to thicken the gravy nicely. This can be made a day in advance and refrigerated.

MAKES 20 SERVINGS
(5 CUPS)

2 cups boiling water
1 cup dried wild mushrooms
8 tablespoons unbleached all-purpose flour
1 medium onion, finely chopped
1 tablespoon vegetable oil
3 cups vegetable stock
1 cup walnuts, toasted and finely chopped
1 teaspoon salt
$\frac{1}{2}$ teaspoon freshly ground black pepper
$\frac{1}{4}$ teaspoon dried thyme

In a bowl, pour boiling water over mushrooms. Let steep 20 minutes.

In a nonstick skillet over medium-high heat, brown flour, stirring constantly, until color is deep amber, about 3 minutes. Be careful not to burn. Scrape flour onto plate to cool.

In a skillet, sauté onion in oil until translucent, about 3 minutes. Set aside.

Drain mushrooms, reserving liquid. Rinse mushrooms to remove all sand and grit. Chop finely. Strain reserved steeping liquid through a paper coffee filter to remove sand.

In a 3-quart saucepan, combine flour with a little stock, whisking until smooth. Add remaining stock and mushroom liquid. Cook over medium heat, whisking constantly until thickened. Add mushrooms, onion, walnuts, salt, pepper and thyme. Cook until heated through, about 5 minutes.

VARIATION: *Substitute 8 ounces finely chopped fresh mushrooms, sautéed in 1 tablespoon oil until browned, for dried mushrooms. Increase vegetable stock to 1 quart.*

Per Serving: 64 Calories; 2g Protein; 4g Fat; 5g Carbohydrates; 0mg Cholesterol; 126mg Sodium; 1g Fiber.

Mushroom Sauce

This is a basic mushroom sauce that can be served over rice, egg noodles, pasta, potatoes, tofu, etc.

MAKES 4 SERVINGS
(2 CUPS)

1 teaspoon olive oil
1 large onion, sliced
4 cloves garlic, crushed
1 pound assorted mushrooms, sliced
$^1/_2$ cup chopped fresh cilantro
1 teaspoon freshly ground black pepper
1 tablespoon vegetarian Worcestershire sauce or $^1/_2$ teaspoon salt
1 cup red wine

Heat oil in a large nonstick skillet over medium-low heat. Add onion and garlic; sauté until soft, about 3 minutes. Add mushrooms and half of cilantro; sauté until mushrooms release most of their liquid, about 10 minutes.

Add pepper, Worcestershire sauce and wine. Sauté until liquid reduces by half, about 20 minutes. Stir in remaining cilantro; sauté 1 minute. Serve immediately over cooked pasta, rice or grain.

Per Serving: 112 Calories; 3g Protein; 2g Fat; 13g Carbohydrates; 0mg Cholesterol; 55mg Sodium; 3g Fiber.

FROM THE HEARTH:
Breads, Biscuits and Muffins

A basket of fresh-baked bread is a welcome sight on any given day, but especially on Thanksgiving. In many ways, bread embodies the wholesome, down-to-earth essence of the Thanksgiving holiday—abundance, a hearty harvest. Sharing a communal bread basket adds warmth and charm to the gathering. Besides, on this mother of all holidays, the extra effort to make bread from scratch is sure to be universally appreciated.

This chapter features an appetizing selection of sweet and savory breads, muffins and biscuits that brings a sense of old-fashioned hospitality and goodness to the Thanksgiving menu. Tempting Boston Brown Bread and Garlic-Herb Bread are great for soaking up soups, dunking in gravies and absorbing the flavors of assertive sauces and salads. Quick breads such as Pumpkin-Apricot Quick Bread and Blue Corn Muffins with Cranberries can either accompany the main course or arrive after dinner with the dessert and hot beverages.

When it comes to baking, patience is a virtue; most breads cannot be whipped up in a jiffy. One kitchen secret is to bake the sweet breads ahead of time, perhaps the night before. This will free up valuable oven space—as well as your hands—and allow you to concentrate on other dishes on the day of your dinner. While there are no strict rules about when to serve bread, be careful not to feed your guests too many loaves before the meal—they'll want to save room for dinner! It's best to stagger the breads throughout the meal rather than introduce them all at once at the very beginning.

Basic Bread Dough

For wheat bread, substitute 2 cups whole-wheat flour for 2 cups unbleached flour. Use this recipe to make homemade Dinner Rolls (recipe follows) for your Thanksgiving guests.

Makes 24 servings
(2 loaves of 12 slices each)

2 cups warm water (95 to 115°F)
1 tablespoon sugar
1/4-ounce package or 1 tablespoon active dry yeast
5 to 6 cups unbleached all-purpose flour, plus additional for kneading
1 tablespoon salt
Cornmeal for dusting baking sheet

If you do not have a candy or instant-read thermometer to test water temperature, drop water on the inside of your wrist to test. It should feel warm but not hot. In a large bowl, combine water, sugar and yeast. Let stand until tiny bubbles begin to appear on surface, about 5 minutes.

Stir in 3 cups flour and the salt. Beat vigorously with a wooden spoon for 2 minutes. Gradually add remaining flour, 1/4 cup at a time, until dough begins to hold together and pull away from sides of bowl. Turn dough out onto a lightly floured work surface and flatten slightly.

Knead bread as follows: Pull far side of dough toward you to fold in half. With heels of hands, push dough away from you. Repeat 2 or 3 times. Rotate dough one-quarter turn and knead 2 to 3 times again. Repeat kneading sequence until dough is smooth and elastic, 8 to 10 minutes. As you knead, replenish surface with flour as necessary.

Put dough in a large oiled bowl. Turn to coat entire ball of dough with oil. Cover bowl with a damp kitchen towel or piece of oiled plastic wrap, oiled side facing the dough. Let dough rise in a warm place (75 to 85°F is ideal) until doubled in size, 1 to 2 hours. (To test for proper rising, poke two fingers into dough. If indentations remain and dough does not spring back, it is ready.)

Meanwhile, lightly oil a baking sheet and sprinkle with cornmeal. Set aside.

Punch dough to deflate it, turn out onto lightly floured surface and knead briefly. (At this point a second rising is optional. It will result in a finer texture and take about half the time of first rising. For second rising, return dough to oiled bowl, let rise until doubled, turn out, punch down and knead briefly.)

Divide dough in half. Shape each half into a smooth ball and place on prepared baking sheet, leaving several inches of space between halves. Flatten each ball into a 6-inch-diameter circle. Cover loaves with a damp towel or oiled plastic wrap and let rise in a warm place until doubled in size, about 1 hour.

Preheat oven to 450°F. With a sharp knife, cut 3 or 4 diagonal slashes in loaves, about ¼ inch deep and 2 inches apart. Put a small pan of water in bottom of oven. Bake loaves about 30 minutes, until golden. To test for doneness, tap bottom of loaf. If it sounds hollow, it is done. For a softer crust, remove bread as soon it's baked. For a crisper crust, turn off oven after bread has finished baking and leave loaves inside with door closed for 5 to 10 additional minutes. Cool on a wire rack.

 Per Serving: 98 Calories; 3g Protein; 1g Fat; 20g Carbohydrates; 0mg Cholesterol; 291mg Sodium; 1g Fiber.

Dinner Rolls

This recipe uses one-half of the Basic Bread recipe. Instructions begin after the dough has risen once, been punched down and been kneaded briefly.

MAKES 16 ROLLS

Lightly oil a baking sheet; set aside. With lightly floured hands, divide dough into 16 equal pieces. Roll each piece into a ball and place 2 inches apart on prepared baking sheet. Cover rolls and let rise in a warm place until doubled in size, 30 to 60 minutes. Bake at 400°F until golden, about 15 to 20 minutes.

 Per Roll: 73 Calories; 2g Protein; 0g Fat; 15g Carbohydrates; 0mg Cholesterol; 219mg Sodium; 1g Fiber.

Orange-Oat Muffins

Oats, oranges and apricots are wonderful companions. Try the soft, luscious Turkish apricots in these. If you use a drier type, be sure to soak or steam them first.

MAKES 10 MUFFINS

⅔ cup rolled (old-fashioned) oats
1 cup whole-wheat pastry flour
⅓ cup unbleached all-purpose flour
1 teaspoon baking soda
¼ teaspoon salt
¼ teaspoon ground cinnamon
1 large egg
⅔ cup milk or soymilk
⅓ cup fresh orange juice
1 teaspoon grated orange zest
¼ cup maple syrup
2 tablespoons vegetable oil
½ cup chopped unsulfured dried apricots (optional)

Preheat oven to 400°F. Grease 10 standard-size muffin pan cups. Set aside.

In a food processor, process oats until coarsely ground. In a medium bowl, mix ground oats, flours, baking soda, salt and cinnamon. In a separate bowl, whisk egg, then add milk, orange juice, orange zest, maple syrup and oil. Stir in apricots if desired.

Make a well in center of dry ingredients and add liquid. Stir just until batter is blended evenly.

Spoon batter into prepared cups, filling each about three-quarters full. Bake 20 minutes or until cake tester inserted into center comes out clean. Cool in pan on a wire rack for 5 minutes. Loosen muffins from cups, remove from pan to rack and cool completely.

🍂 Per Muffin: 161 Calories; 5g Protein; 5g Fat; 26g Carbohydrates; 23mg Cholesterol; 200mg Sodium; 3g Fiber.

Garlic-Herb Bread

This garlic bread is best served right out of the oven, so make sure you plan for this.

Makes 8 servings
(8 slices)

1 stick (½ cup) butter or margarine, softened
2 to 4 cloves garlic, minced
2 tablespoons chopped fresh chives
2 tablespoons chopped fresh parsley
1 loaf French bread (baguette)

Preheat oven to 400°F. In a food processor, combine butter or margarine, garlic, chives and parsley. Process until smooth and well blended.

Cut bread, almost through to the crust, into slices about 1 inch thick. Spread garlic butter in slits. Wrap bread in foil (if necessary, cut loaf in half and wrap each half separately).

Bake 20 minutes. For a crisp, golden crust, unwrap loaf for last 5 to 10 minutes of baking time.

Per Serving: 123 Calories; 2g Protein; 7g Fat; 13g Carbohydrates; 16mg Cholesterol; 214mg Sodium; 1g Fiber.

Apple Focaccia

For a perfectly golden crust, bake this in a cast-iron skillet. For the best flavor (and to give you one fewer thing to do on The Big Day), make it a day in advance to give the flavors a chance to meld.

Makes 8 servings

Dough
1 small apple, cored and quartered
2 cups unbleached white flour, plus about 2 tablespoons for kneading
$\frac{1}{4}$ teaspoon cinnamon
1 tablespoon sugar or 2 teaspoons honey
1 scant teaspoon quick-rising yeast
$\frac{1}{4}$ to $\frac{1}{2}$ teaspoon salt (optional)
1 tablespoon soy margarine (optional)
$\frac{1}{3}$ to $\frac{1}{2}$ cup hot tap water
$\frac{1}{3}$ cup raisins

Filling
4 medium apples
Juice of $\frac{1}{2}$ lemon
Pinch freshly ground white pepper
Pinch ground cloves
Pinch ground cardamom
Pinch grated nutmeg
Pinch ground ginger or $\frac{1}{2}$ teaspoon grated ginger root
1 teaspoon vanilla extract
$\frac{1}{4}$ to $\frac{1}{3}$ cup sugar or honey
$\frac{1}{4}$ to $\frac{1}{2}$ cup brown sugar or 2 tablespoons blackstrap molasses
1 teaspoon cornstarch (2 teaspoons if using honey instead of sugar)

Glaze
2 tablespoons apricot jam or preserves
1 teaspoon water

To make the dough, process quartered apple in a food processor for about 20 seconds; transfer to a separate bowl. Put 2 cups flour, cinnamon, sugar or honey, yeast and salt if desired in food processor; process 5 seconds. Add processed apple and margarine if desired; process an additional 5 seconds. With processor running, gradually add $\frac{1}{3}$ cup hot water through feeder tube. Stop machine and let dough rest about 20 seconds. Continue processing and adding water gradually through feeder tube until dough forms a soft ball and sides of bowl are clean. Pulse 2 or 3 more times. Sprinkle raisins and 1 tablespoon flour onto a clean surface. Turn out dough onto surface and knead about 1 minute to incorporate raisins. Add flour if dough is very sticky. Lightly flour inside of a plastic bag. Place dough in bag, seal and let rest 15 to 20 minutes in a warm dark place.

Roll dough into a circle 12 to 14 inches in diameter. Lay in oiled skillet or baking dish. Cover with a kitchen towel and set aside in a warm place while you prepare filling. Preheat oven to 400°F.

To make the filling, core and slice apples paper thin. Sprinkle lemon juice over apple slices. Add remaining ingredients and mix well. Spoon filling into dough. Bake 20 minutes, then rotate pan 180 degrees. Reduce oven temperature to 375°F and bake an additional 20 minutes, or until apples are browned. Cool in pan 5 minutes. Remove from pan and cool thoroughly on wire rack.

To make the glaze, in a small saucepan, melt jam or preserves. Add water and bring to a boil, stirring vigorously. Brush glaze over apples and serve.

🍃 Per Serving: 256 Calories; 3.6g Protein; 2g Fat; 58g Carbohydrates; 0mg Cholesterol; 7mg Sodium; 3g Fiber.

Ken's Blue Cornbread

This recipe give cornbread a twist by using blue instead of yellow cornmeal.

2 tablespoons vegetable oil
1 small onion, minced
1½ cups blue cornmeal
½ cup whole-wheat pastry flour
3 teaspoons baking powder
¾ teaspoon salt
1 teaspoon dried sage
1 teaspoon dried thyme
2 eggs, beaten
2 tablespoons honey
1 cup milk or soymilk

Preheat oven to 475°F. Place an ungreased 9-inch cast-iron skillet in oven to heat up. Heat oil in another pan, sauté onions and set aside. Combine dry ingredients, including herbs, in a bowl. Combine eggs, honey and milk in another bowl. Combine wet and dry ingredients and fold in onions. Carefully remove heated skillet from oven. Pour in batter, return to oven and bake 20 minutes, or until the top springs back when pressed.

Per Serving: 197 Calories; 5g Protein; 7g Fat; 30g Carbohydrates; 57mg Cholesterol; 407mg Sodium; 2g Fiber.

Easy Drop Biscuits

Drop biscuits go right from mixing to baking, eliminating the steps of rolling and cutting. As with all quick breads, mix lightly for tender biscuits. Overmixing develops gluten, resulting in tough biscuits.

MAKES 12 LARGE BISCUITS

1 cup sifted whole-wheat or white wheat flour
1 cup sifted unbleached all-purpose flour
1 tablespoon baking powder
$\frac{1}{2}$ teaspoon salt
$\frac{1}{3}$ cup canola oil
1 cup reconstituted powdered nonfat milk or powdered soymilk

Preheat oven to 400°F. Combine flours, baking powder and salt in a sifter or wire-meshed sieve. Sift together into a large bowl.

In a separate small bowl, combine oil and milk or soymilk. Whisk to mix and pour into flour mixture. Stir with a fork or fold with a rubber spatula until just mixed and dough holds together (do not overmix).

Drop dough by heaping tablespoons at least 1 inch apart onto a lightly oiled baking sheet. Bake until biscuits are golden brown on top, 10 to 12 minutes. Remove to a napkin-lined basket. Serve hot.

HELPFUL HINT: *To measure flour accurately, sift more flour than you need onto a large sheet of waxed paper. Spoon lightly into a 1-cup measure that can be leveled with a flat-edged knife or spatula. Gather up opposite edges of waxed paper and pour excess flour back into the bag.*

🍂 Per Biscuit: 130 Calories; 3g Protein; 6g Fat; 15g Carbohydrates; 1mg Cholesterol; 222mg Sodium; 1g Fiber.

Half-Wheat Biscuits

Whole-wheat flour is denser than white flour, so this recipe uses not only baking powder for leavening but also a little quick-rising yeast to give the biscuits a boost. Be sure your biscuit cutter is sharp, and cut straight down for a sharp edge; don't twist. If the biscuit edges are compressed by twisting the cutter, the biscuits won't rise as high.

MAKES ABOUT 15 BISCUITS

1 cup sifted whole-wheat flour or white wheat flour
1 cup sifted unbleached white flour
1 tablespoon baking powder
1 teaspoon salt
³/₄ cup warm (120°F) reconstituted powdered nonfat milk or reconstituted
    powdered soymilk
1 teaspoon quick-rising active dry yeast
¹/₃ cup canola oil
1 tablespoon honey

Preheat oven to 400°F. Combine flours, baking powder and salt in a sifter or wire-meshed sieve. Sift together into a large bowl.

In a smaller bowl, add milk or soymilk. Sprinkle yeast over surface. Whisk to mix and dissolve. Dip tablespoon into oil. Measure honey into tablespoon. Add to yeast-milk mixture along with oil. Whisk to mix and dissolve honey.

Add wet mixture to flour mixture. Stir with a fork or fold with a rubber spatula until just mixed and dough holds together (do not overmix). Turn out onto a lightly floured board. Roll out ½-inch thick. Cut biscuits straight down with a 2-inch cutter. Gather up dough scraps, reroll and cut, handling dough as little and lightly as possible.

Bake 1 inch apart on an ungreased baking sheet until biscuits have risen and are golden brown on top, 10 to 12 minutes. Serve hot.

🌿 Per Biscuit: 110 Calories; 2g Protein; 5g Fat; 14g Carbohydrates; 1mg Cholesterol; 247mg Sodium; 1g Fiber.

White Wheat Bread

This bread uses the sponge method, a preliminary rising using all the liquid and half the flour. It can also be made in a large-capacity food processor or a large kitchen mixer equipped with a dough hook.

Makes 12 servings
(1 loaf of 12 slices)

1¼ cups lukewarm water
¼-ounce packet active dry yeast
1½ cups white wheat flour, leveled but not sifted
1½ cups unbleached all-purpose flour, leveled but not sifted
1 teaspoon salt
Additional unbleached all-purpose flour for kneading

Put water in a large bowl. Sprinkle yeast over surface. Let soften. Whisk to dissolve. Add half of each of the flours and salt; stir to mix. Cover with a clean, damp tea towel. Let rise in a warm (85°F) place until doubled in bulk, up to 1 hour.

Stir down. Add remaining flours, stirring with a sturdy wooden or stainless steel spoon to incorporate. Turn out on a board lightly floured with unbleached all-purpose flour. Knead 5 to 8 minutes until dough is smooth, elastic and not sticky.

Wash and dry mixing bowl; oil lightly. Return dough to bowl. Cover with a damp towel. Let rise in a warm (85°F) place until doubled in bulk, about 1 hour.

Punch down dough, turn out on board and shape into a loaf. Place in a lightly oiled loaf pan. Cover with a damp towel. Let rise until doubled in size or until impression made with thumb does not spring back.

Preheat oven to 400°F. Make 3 diagonal slashes ¼-inch deep on top with a straight-edge razor blade or sharp knife. Bake 35 to 40 minutes. Turn out on a wire rack to cool.

VARIATIONS:

- *If using a heavy-duty mixer with dough attachment, add water and yeast to mixer bowl as directed. Use whisk or paddle attachment to mix up sponge. Let rise in mixer bowl covered with a damp towel. Use dough hook to incorporate remaining flour. Knead in bowl with dough hook 5 to 8 minutes. Proceed as directed.*

- *If using a food processor, put all flours and salt in bowl of a large-capacity (at least 7 cups) food processor fitted with dough blade or steel blade. Dissolve yeast in ¼ cup lukewarm water. Stir into 1 cup cold water in a large measuring cup. (Add dissolved yeast to cold water because action of food processor heats up dough.)*

With motor running, pour liquid into flours in food processor bowl and process until dough forms a ball. Continue to process 1 minute. Remove dough from processor bowl carefully, scraping sides and blade. Follow recipe instructions starting with second rising.

Per Serving: 123 Calories; 4g Protein; 1g Fat; 27g Carbohydrates; 0mg Cholesterol; 178mg Sodium; 1g Fiber.

Corn Batter Bread

This delicious bread recipe makes 2 loaves. You can freeze the second loaf for up to 3 months. Make sure it has cooled completely and double wrap it before freezing.

MAKES 24 SERVINGS
(2 LOAVES OF 12 SLICES EACH)

Two $^1/_4$-ounce packets active dry yeast
$^1/_2$ cup nonfat dry milk
$1^1/_2$ cups warm (110°F) water
$1^1/_2$ teaspoons salt
$^1/_4$ cup sugar
3 tablespoons corn oil, preferably cold-pressed
3 cups bread flour
$1^1/_2$ cups cornmeal
2 cups corn kernels

In a large bowl, stir yeast and dry milk into warm water, whisking to dissolve. Add salt, sugar and oil, whisking to mix. With a large spoon, stir in flour and cornmeal. Mix in bowl of a kitchen mixer with dough hooks 1 to 2 minutes, or knead by hand on a lightly floured surface 1 to 2 minutes. While mixing or kneading, fold in corn kernels.

Divide batter into 2 lightly oiled or nonstick 8-by-4-inch loaf pans. Cover with lightly oiled wax paper and let rise in a warm place until doubled, at least 1 hour. Bread is ready to bake when dough holds indentation left by lightly pressing with finger.

Bake at 400°F until browned and a wooden pick inserted in center comes out dry, about 35 minutes. Remove loaves from pans and place on wire racks to cool.

Per Serving: 138 Calories; 4g Protein; 2g Fat; 25g Carbohydrates; 1mg Cholesterol; 148mg Sodium; 2g Fiber.

Blue Corn Muffins with Cranberries

These tart muffins combine foods native to America: corn and cranberries.

MAKES ABOUT 10 MUFFINS

$^3/_4$ cup finely ground blue cornmeal
1 cup unbleached white flour
2 teaspoons baking powder
1 teaspoon baking soda
Pinch salt
1 egg plus 1 egg white
$^3/_4$ cup skim milk
$^1/_3$ cup canola oil
$^1/_2$ cup honey or maple syrup
3 ounces cranberries (about $^3/_4$ cup)

Preheat oven to 350°F. Stir together dry ingredients in a large bowl. In a separate bowl, combine egg and egg white, milk, oil and honey or maple syrup. Pour wet ingredients into dry ingredients; mix just until combined (overmixing will result in a tough texture). Fold in cranberries. Fill oiled muffin tins or paper muffin liners about ¾ full with batter. Bake until tester inserted in muffin center comes out clean, 18 to 20 minutes.

Per Muffin: 215 Calories; 4g Protein; 8g Fat; 33g Carbohydrates; 22mg Cholesterol; 238mg Sodium; 1g Fiber.

Four-Grain Cornbread

Cornbread is usually a quick bread, but this yeasted version is flavorful and worth the rising time.

MAKES ABOUT 12 SERVINGS
(1 LOAF OF 12 SLICES)

½ cup millet
¾ cup hot tap water
1 package dry yeast
½ teaspoon honey (optional)
1⅓ cups warm water
½ cup corn flour
1 cup whole-wheat bread flour
1½ cups unbleached white flour
2 teaspoons salt
3 tablespoons rolled oats

Place millet in a small bowl; cover with ¾ cup hot tap water. Set aside until millet softens and absorbs water, about 15 minutes. In a separate small bowl or cup, dissolve yeast and honey (if desired) in 1⅓ cups warm water; set aside until foamy.

In a large bowl, combine flours and salt. Add yeast mixture; knead until mixture is incorporated, about 2 minutes. Drain millet and add to dough. Knead about 10 minutes, until millet is evenly incorporated. (Dough will be somewhat sticky.)

Lightly oil a large bowl. Place dough in bowl; immediately turn dough over so that oiled side is up. Cover with a damp towel and let rise until doubled in bulk, 2 to 3 hours.

Punch down dough; shape into a round loaf. Place loaf on a floured peel or baking sheet. Sprinkle oats on top, pressing down lightly to stick to dough. Let rise until almost doubled in bulk, about 1 hour.

Place bread-baking tiles or baking sheet into oven; preheat to 450°F. Slash top of loaf decoratively and slide onto heated tiles or baking sheet. Bake until top is well browned and bread sounds hollow when tapped on bottom, about 30 to 45 minutes.

Per Serving: 150 Calories; 5g Protein; 1g Fat; 30g Carbohydrates; 0mg Cholesterol; 389mg Sodium; 3g Fiber.

Zucchini Cornbread

Creating a low-fat, moist cornbread is not impossible. In this recipe, zucchini provides the moisture.

MAKES 12 SERVINGS

1 cup yellow cornmeal
1 cup unbleached white flour
⅓ cup sugar
1 tablespoon baking powder
½ teaspoon salt
1 egg, beaten, plus 1 egg white
1 cup buttermilk
2 tablespoons vegetable oil
1 cup fresh or thawed frozen corn kernels
1 cup shredded zucchini

Preheat oven to 375°F. Combine cornmeal, flour, sugar, baking powder and salt in a mixing bowl. In a separate bowl, beat egg and egg white; whisk in buttermilk and oil. Gently fold liquid ingredients into dry ingredients until batter is formed. Fold in corn and zucchini.

Pour batter into a lightly greased 8-inch-square baking pan or muffin pan. Bake until crust is golden brown and a toothpick inserted in center comes out clean, about 20 to 25 minutes. Serve warm.

Per Serving: 143 Calories; 4g Protein; 3g Fat; 25g Carbohydrates; 18mg Cholesterol; 228mg Sodium; 1g Fiber.

Super Grain Cornbread

Quinoa transforms cornbread into a nutrient-rich treat. Serve with 15-Bean and Winter Squash Chili (see recipe page 89).

(see recipe page 89).

MAKES 8 SERVINGS

1/2 cup quinoa, rinsed
1 cup water
1 cup yellow cornmeal
1 cup unbleached all-purpose flour
1/3 cup sugar
1 tablespoon baking powder
1/2 teaspoon salt
1 large egg plus 1 large egg white, beaten
1 cup low-fat milk or soymilk
1/3 cup canola oil
2 green onions (white and pale green parts), chopped
1/2 cup chopped red bell pepper
11-ounce can corn kernels, drained

In a small saucepan, combine quinoa and water, and bring to a simmer over medium-high heat. Reduce heat, cover and simmer until quinoa is tender and liquid is absorbed, 13 to 15 minutes. Remove from heat and fluff grains with a fork. Cover and set aside for 10 to 15 minutes.

Meanwhile, preheat oven to 375°F degrees. Lightly grease a 9-inch round baking pan. In a medium bowl, mix cornmeal, flour, sugar, baking powder and salt. In a separate bowl, whisk together eggs, egg whites, milk, oil, green onions, bell pepper and corn. Add liquid ingredients to dry ingredients and mix until blended. Fold in quinoa.

Pour batter into prepared pan. Bake until top is lightly browned and a toothpick inserted into center comes out clean, 20 to 25 minutes. Remove to a wire rack, let cool 10 minutes and cut into wedges.

Per Serving: 288 Calories; 7g Protein; 11g Fat; 39g Carbohydrates; 28mg Cholesterol; 455mg Sodium; 2g Fiber.

Pumpkin-Spice Muffins

If you're skipping the pumpkin pie for dessert, here's a great way to add that traditional taste to your Thanksgiving meal. These muffins are especially good served warm.

MAKES 12 MUFFINS

1¾ cups whole-wheat pastry flour or unbleached white flour
1 teaspoon baking powder
½ teaspoon baking soda
¼ teaspoon salt
1 teaspoon ground cinnamon
¾ cup fresh, cooked pumpkin or canned pumpkin
⅔ cup low-fat buttermilk
2 tablespoons canola oil
½ cup honey
2 egg whites, lightly beaten

Preheat oven to 400°F. Line a 12-cup muffin tin with muffin papers. In a large bowl, sift together flour, baking powder, baking soda, salt and cinnamon. In another bowl, stir together remaining ingredients. Combine contents of two bowls, stirring until just blended. Divide batter equally among 12 muffin cups. Bake 20 minutes, or until muffins are springy to the touch and lightly browned.

Per Muffin: 136 Calories; 4g Protein; 3g Fat; 24g Carbohydrates; 1mg Cholesterol; 140mg Sodium; 3g Fiber.

Breadsticks

There's no such thing as an imperfect breadstick. If one stick is too long for the pan, simply bend 1 end over to fit, like a shepherd's crook. What a different addition to the Thanksgiving table, and a treat for the children!

1 recipe Fast Pizza Dough, mixed, kneaded and risen (recipe follows)

Preheat oven to 500°F. Turn out risen dough onto a lightly floured surface. Roll out into a rectangle roughly 12 by 16 inches, dusting top with flour lightly as needed to prevent sticking.

With a knife, score dough in half with cut parallel to 12-inch side. Score each half in half again in the same direction. Score each quarter in half again in the same direction. Score each eighth in half again in the same direction (you should have 16 strips, about 1 inch wide and 12 inches long).

Cut through each strip with a serrated knife. Lift strips individually; cut in half crosswise. Quickly twist and pull half strips to form a twisted rope about 10 inches long. Repeat until all strips are cut and twisted.

Lay strips side by side vertically in three 11½-by-17-inch lightly oiled baking pans. Bake until breadsticks are golden brown, about 15 minutes. Cool on rack.

> **HELPFUL HINTS:** *Electric ovens tend to cook faster; these recipes were tested in a gas oven. You may need to lower the heat of an electric oven to 450°F. If your oven won't hold 3 large baking pans, use a 10½-by-15½-inch size. Still not enough room? Put 1 pan in the refrigerator covered with lightly oiled waxed paper, oiled side down, until other pans are baked.*

Per Breadstick: 40 Calories; 1g Protein; 0g Fat; 8g Carbohydrates; 0mg Cholesterol; 67mg Sodium; 0g Fiber.

Fast Pizza Dough

Fast-rising yeast and one-bowl mixing and kneading has this dough ready to roll, top and bake in 20 minutes. Hot water—120 to 130°F—gives fast-rising yeast its get-up-and-go. The water will feel hot to the touch. Until you've memorized the feel, use a thermometer. Do not knead dough for pizza after first rising; it will be harder to roll out.

MAKES ONE 14-INCH ROUND (8 WEDGES)
OR 10½-BY-15½-INCH RECTANGULAR
THICK-CRUST PIZZA, TWO 14-INCH ROUND
THIN-CRUST PIZZAS OR 32 BREADSTICKS

1¼ cups hot (120 to 130°F) water
¼-ounce packet rapid-rising active dry yeast
1 teaspoon salt
3 tablespoons toasted wheat germ
3 cups all-purpose unbleached white flour, leveled but not sifted,
    plus additional flour for kneading

Preheat oven to 500°F. Pour water into a medium bowl; sprinkle in yeast. Stir with a wire whisk to dissolve quickly. Add salt and wheat germ; whisk again.

Add 3 cups flour. With a sturdy wooden or stainless steel spoon, stir until dough forms a mass and leaves sides of bowl. Knead dough briefly in bowl, sprinkling in extra flour until dough is smooth and not sticky but still soft, about 3 minutes.

Set bowl in a pie pan. Pour 2 cups hot water into pie pan. Cover bowl with lightly oiled waxed paper, oiled side down, or a damp kitchen towel. Let rise 15 minutes.

Turn out with a spatula onto a floured board (do not knead). Roll out into desired shape.

HELPFUL HINT: *To measure flour without wasting any, place measuring cup on a waxed paper square. Scoop flour in, letting it fall on paper. Level off with a straight-edge spatula or back of a knife. Use flour on waxed paper for kneading dough and dusting on surface to roll out dough. Any unused flour can be gathered up in waxed paper and poured back into flour container.*

🔖 Per ⅛ Recipe: 162 Calories; 6g Protein; 1g Fat; 33g Carbohydrates; 0mg Cholesterol; 267mg Sodium; 2g Fiber.

Apple-Cheddar Muffins

This is a great dinner muffin.

2 cups unbleached white flour
1 tablespoon plus 1 teaspoon baking powder
$1/2$ teaspoon kosher salt or regular salt
3 tablespoons brown sugar
$1/2$ teaspoon ground allspice
$3/4$ cup grated low-fat Cheddar cheese
2 eggs, lightly beaten, or equivalent Egg Replacer
1 cup soy, rice or dairy milk
3 tablespoons canola oil
$1/2$ cup applesauce

Preheat oven to 400°F. Line a 12-cup muffin pan with paper muffin cups or oil, or spray with cooking spray; set aside.

In a large mixing bowl, combine flour, baking powder, salt, brown sugar, allspice and cheese. In a separate bowl, combine remaining ingredients.

Make a well in center of dry ingredients; pour in wet ingredients all at once. Blend until combined, leaving no dry spots; do not overmix. Fill muffin cups and bake 20 minutes. Serve warm.

Per Muffin: 195 Calories; 7g Protein; 7g Fat; 25g Carbohydrates; 48mg Cholesterol; 336mg Sodium; 1g Fiber.

Boston Molasses Muffins

These are reminiscent of Boston brown bread, but with a lighter molasses taste.

$1\frac{1}{2}$ cups unbleached white flour
$\frac{1}{2}$ cup yellow cornmeal
$\frac{1}{4}$ cup dark brown sugar
1 teaspoon baking soda
1 cup soy, rice or dairy milk
1 tablespoon cider vinegar
$\frac{1}{4}$ cup molasses
2 tablespoons canola oil
2 tablespoons applesauce
$\frac{1}{2}$ cup currants or raisins
1 egg, lightly beaten, or equivalent Egg Replacer

Preheat oven to 400°F. Line a 12-cup muffin pan with paper muffin cups, or oil or spray with cooking spray; set aside.

In a medium mixing bowl, combine flour, cornmeal, sugar and baking soda. In a separate bowl, mix remaining ingredients. Make a well in center of dry ingredients; pour in liquid ingredients all at once. Blend until well combined, leaving no dry spots; do not overmix.

Fill muffin cups about ¾ full. Bake until tops spring back when lightly pressed, about 20 minutes. Cool on rack 5 minutes before serving.

Per Muffin: 197 Calories; 4g Protein; 4g Fat; 36g Carbohydrates; 21mg Cholesterol; 143mg Sodium; 1g Fiber.

Chestnut and Corn Patties

These patties were considered bread by Native Americans and were baked on a hot stone. The dough was sometimes wrapped in corn husks and steamed like a tamale.

MAKES 6 SERVINGS

½ cup stone-ground cornmeal
1 cup water
3 tablespoons vegetable oil for frying
1 cup finely diced onion
2 cloves garlic, minced
1 pound chestnuts, roasted, peeled and pureed, or 15.5-ounce can unsweet-
    ened chestnut puree
Salt and freshly ground black pepper to taste

Slowly add cornmeal to boiling water; cook until thick. (Cornmeal should hold form when scooped out of pan.) Heat 1 tablespoon oil in a small skillet; sauté onion and garlic until transparent. Add onion and garlic to cornmeal along with chestnut puree. Mix well; form into 6 patties.

Place heavy skillet over medium heat; add remaining oil. Add patties; fry 5 minutes on each side. Season with salt and pepper.

Per Serving: 249 Calories; 6g Protein; 4g Fat; 50g Carbohydrates; 0mg Cholesterol; 8mg Sodium; 1g Fiber.

Sweet Potato Cakes

Sweet potatoes were used often by Native Americans. They were baked in ashes, added to stews and made into unleavened breads. The eggs would have been wild bird or duck eggs.

4 large sweet potatoes
3 eggs, beaten
1 cup flour
1$\frac{1}{2}$ teaspoons salt
2 tablespoons vegetable oil

Preheat oven to 350°F. Bake sweet potatoes until tender; peel and mash. When cool, add eggs, flour and salt.

Heat griddle; brush with oil. Drop batter by large spoonfuls onto griddle. Fry cakes 3 to 4 minutes or until golden brown. Flip and cook other side 3 to 4 minutes. Keep cakes warm until serving time.

 Per Serving: 207 Calories; 5g Protein; 6g Fat; 34g Carbohydrates; 80mg Cholesterol; 462mg Sodium; 4g Fiber.

Hot Corn Sticks

If you don't have cast-iron "corn-stick" pans, bake these little cornbreads in mini-muffin pans. Either way, they will delight the children among your guests.

MAKES 14 STICKS
(24 MINI-MUFFINS)

1 cup unbleached white flour
¾ cup cornmeal
¼ cup sugar
2 teaspoons baking powder
¼ teaspoon salt
¾ cup skim milk or soymilk
¼ cup canola oil
1 egg, lightly beaten

Preheat oven to 450°F. Generously spray 2 cast-iron "corn-stick" pans with cooking spray.

In a medium bowl, sift flour with cornmeal, sugar, baking powder and salt. Add milk or soymilk, oil and egg. Stir with a fork until just blended. Do not overmix. Fill pans ¾ full.

Bake about 20 minutes, until golden brown. Serve immediately, or remove from pan, cool and wrap tightly in foil. Reheat before serving.

Per Stick: 111 Calories; 3g Protein; 4g Fat; 15g Carbohydrates; 20mg Cholesterol; 114mg Sodium; 1g Fiber.

Per Mini-Muffin: 65 Calories; 2g Protein; 2g Fat; 9g Carbohydrates; 12mg Cholesterol; 67mg Sodium; 0g Fiber.

Sweet Potato Cornbread

What could be more American and more appropriate for Thanksgiving than cornbread sweetened and made moist by sweet potatoes?

MAKES ABOUT 16 SERVINGS
(16 SLICES)

$^{3}/_{4}$ cup yellow or white cornmeal
$^{3}/_{4}$ cup unbleached white flour
1 tablespoon baking powder
Pinch cinnamon, or to taste
Pinch cardamom, or to taste
$^{1}/_{2}$ teaspoon salt
$^{1}/_{2}$ cup margarine or butter
$^{1}/_{4}$ cup brown sugar
1 egg plus 1 egg white
1 tablespoon fresh orange juice
1 cup cooked mashed sweet potato
$^{1}/_{4}$ to $^{1}/_{2}$ cup skim milk or nondairy milk
$^{1}/_{2}$ cup frozen corn kernels, thawed
4-ounce can green chilies, rinsed and chopped

Preheat oven to 350°F. Combine dry ingredients in a large mixing bowl.

With an electric mixer, cream margarine or butter until fluffy, about 1 minute. Add brown sugar and mix briefly. Add egg and egg white, orange juice, sweet potato and milk. Mix until smooth.

Add dry ingredients; mix well. Fold in corn and green chilies. Pour batter into two 9-inch pie pans coated with cooking spray. Bake until firm and until cake tester inserted in center comes out clean, about 20 minutes. Cool before serving.

Per Serving: 121 Calories; 2g Protein; 6g Fat; 16g Carbohydrates; 10mg Cholesterol; 322mg Sodium; 1g Fiber.

Pumpkin-Apricot Quick Bread

Dried apricots limit the fat and calories in this recipe, and provide a delightful flavor and texture.

Makes 15 servings
(1 loaf of 15 slices)

1^3/$_4$ cups all-purpose flour
1 teaspoon baking soda
^{1}/$_2$ teaspoon baking powder
^{1}/$_2$ teaspoon salt
^{1}/$_4$ teaspoon cinnamon
^{1}/$_4$ teaspoon ground ginger
^{1}/$_4$ teaspoon ground cardamom
^{1}/$_4$ teaspoon ground coriander
1 cup sugar
^{1}/$_2$ cup coarsely chopped dried apricots
15-ounce can pumpkin puree
1 tablespoon Egg Replacer, dissolved in 4 tablespoons water, or 2 eggs
^{1}/$_3$ cup fresh orange juice
1 tablespoon grated orange zest

Preheat oven to 350°F. Lightly grease and flour a 9-by-5-by-3-inch loaf pan.

In a large bowl, combine flour, baking soda, baking powder, salt, cinnamon, ginger, cardamom, coriander, sugar and apricots; mix thoroughly.

In another bowl, whisk together pumpkin puree, Egg Replacer or eggs, orange juice and zest. Pour pumpkin mixture over dry ingredients; stir until batter is well blended.

Transfer batter to loaf pan; bake until tester inserted in center comes out clean, 55 to 60 minutes.

HELPFUL HINT: *Tent loaf with foil to avoid overbrowning halfway through baking, if necessary.*

Per Serving: 143 Calories; 2g Protein; 0g Fat; 34g Carbohydrates; 0mg Cholesterol; 223mg Sodium; 2g Fiber.

Pumpkin Bread

This delicious yeast-risen pumpkin bread is a welcome alternative to sweet, rich, quick pumpkin breads. It also makes fine sandwiches and fabulous toast.

MAKES ABOUT 12 SERVINGS
(1 LOAF OF 12 SLICES)

¼-ounce pkg. active dry yeast (about 1 tablespoon)
½ cup warm water (110°F)
1 teaspoon salt
2 teaspoons caraway seed
2 tablespoons molasses (not blackstrap)
1 cup fresh or canned pumpkin puree
3 cups unbleached all-purpose flour, plus additional flour for kneading

Preheat oven to 400°F.

In a large bowl, mix yeast and water, stirring to combine and dissolve. Add salt, caraway seed and molasses, stirring to mix.

Add pumpkin puree, stirring to mix. Add 3 cups flour. Stir with a large, sturdy spoon until all flour is incorporated and dough leaves sides of bowl.

Turn out onto a floured surface. Knead until dough is smooth and satiny, about 5 to 8 minutes.

Lightly oil bowl. Return dough to bowl. Cover with a clean, damp tea towel. Set in a warm place (85°F) to rise.

Let rise until doubled, about 1 hour. Punch down and shape into loaf. Place in a lightly oiled bread pan. Cover with a clean, damp tea towel. Let rise until doubled and indentation made with thumb remains.

Bake until browned on top and bottom sounds hollow when tapped, about 35 minutes. Remove from pan. Let cool on a wire rack.

VARIATIONS:

- *Substitute 2 tablespoons brown sugar for molasses, and ½ cup raisins for caraway seed. Add ½ teaspoon cinnamon to liquid ingredients. Substitute whole-wheat or rye flour for ⅓ of the white flour in original recipe.*

- *To make a pumpkin-cinnamon loaf, when dough is punched down, instead of shaping it into a loaf, stretch the dough into a rectangular shape. Sprinkle with a mixture of sugar and cinnamon, then roll dough up from short side to form a loaf. Place in loaf pan and proceed with recipe.*

Per Serving: 130 Calories; 4g Protein; 0g Fat; 28g Carbohydrates; 0mg Cholesterol; 180mg Sodium; 2g Fiber.

Candied Apple Muffins

The candied flavor comes from little cinnamon candies called Red Hots.

MAKES 12 MUFFINS

1½ cups unbleached all-purpose flour
½ cup soy flour
1 tablespoon baking powder
½ teaspoon salt
½ teaspoon ground cinnamon
⅓ cup sugar
2 eggs, equivalent egg substitute or equivalent Egg Replacer
1 cup unsweetened or regular applesauce
4 tablespoons canola oil
¼ cup cinnamon candies

Preheat oven to 375°F. Lightly oil a muffin tin. In a large bowl, combine flours, baking powder, salt, cinnamon and sugar; set aside.

In a medium bowl, lightly beat eggs or Egg Replacer; stir in applesauce and oil. Stir liquids into flour mixture only until dry ingredients are moistened. Add cinnamon candies; fold in quickly to prevent color from bleeding into batter.

Spoon batter into a muffin tin until cups are ⅔ to ¾ full. Bake 25 minutes, or until a toothpick inserted in center comes out clean.

VARIATION: *Omit candies and stir into batter ¼ cup chopped walnuts, pecans, dried cherries or cranberries, golden or dark raisins, dried apples or apricots.*

Per Muffin: 142 Calories; 4g Protein; 4g Fat; 15g Carbohydrates; 28mg Cholesterol; 155mg Sodium; 1g Fiber.

Boston Brown Bread

This dark, rich, moist bread originated in New England, where it was a traditional accompaniment to baked beans. It uses no eggs and no fat. Brown bread improves with age—up to two weeks—wrapped and refrigerated. It is great eaten as is, and just as fine toasted and served with cream cheese or preserves.

MAKES 32 SERVINGS

1 cup unbleached white flour
1 1/2 cups whole-wheat flour
1/2 cup cornmeal
1 1/2 teaspoons baking powder
1 teaspoon baking soda
2 tablespoons packed brown sugar
1/2 teaspoon salt
2 cups buttermilk or reconstituted dry buttermilk powder
1/2 cup molasses
1 cup dark raisins

Lightly oil insides of four 14- to 15-ounce empty clean cans, or two 28- to 29-ounce cans. Cut waxed paper circles to fit bottoms. Lightly oil paper circles; fit paper inside bottoms of cans. Set cans aside.

In a 5-cup sifter, add flours, cornmeal, baking powder, baking soda, brown sugar and salt. Sift together in a large bowl. Add buttermilk, molasses and raisins; stir to mix. Spoon batter 2/3 full into prepared cans.

Cover cans with lightly oiled aluminum foil, oiled side facing batter. Place on rack in a large kettle or stockpot filled with 3 inches boiling water. Steam about 1 hour for small cans, 1 1/2 hours for large cans. Check water level, adding boiling water if necessary. When done, a wooden pick inserted in center will come out clean.

Remove from steamer with tongs; cool in cans on wire rack 5 minutes. Invert can to release loaves, loosening loaves if necessary by running a knife around edges. Let cool to room temperature on wire racks. Wrap loaves tightly in plastic wrap and refrigerate.

To serve, slice loaves with a sharp serrated knife. Serve at room temperature, cold or toasted.

HELPFUL HINT: *Canned beans come in 14- and 15-ounce cans. Canned tomatoes come in 28-ounce cans; canned pumpkin, in 29-ounce cans. Bread also may be steamed in other molds, but the cylindrical shape is traditional.*

VARIATIONS:

- *Substitute 2 cups minus 2 tablespoons reconstituted soymilk powder plus 2 tablespoons cider vinegar for buttermilk.*

- *Substitute ½ cup chopped pitted dates for ½ cup raisins.*

 Per Serving: 74 Calories; 2g Protein; 0g Fat; 17g Carbohydrates; 1mg Cholesterol; 115mg Sodium; 1g Fiber.

HAPPY ENDINGS:
Delicious Desserts

Thanksgiving is one of the rare times when we freely allow ourselves to surrender to temptation, ignore our misgivings and indulge in sweets without apologies or regrets. If only for this one day, Americans across the land join together, elbow-to-elbow, and say goodbye to guilt. Swimsuit season is months away. Skipping the grand finale on Thanksgiving is simply unimaginable.

Just as Christmas is famous for sugar cookies and Valentine's Day is celebrated with chocolate, the classic Thanksgiving dinner culminates in pumpkin pie. November, after all, is pumpkin season. (Even the Pilgrims and Native Americans are said to have shared maple-sweetened pumpkins.) In keeping with this time-honored tradition, this chapter offers an abundance of delicious pumpkin-inspired desserts to whet your appetite, such as Tofu-Pumpkin Pie, Spiced Pumpkin Custard, Vegan Pumpkin Pie, Fresh Pumpkin Pie and many others.

In addition to the revered pumpkin pie, the tangy fruits of autumn—apples, pears and cranberries—inspire a host of cobblers, cakes and crumbles.

Ginger-Poached Pears in Red Wine, Apple-Cranberry Crumb Tart and Corn Apple Cobbler are just some of the fruit-filled recipes featured in this chapter. If you have a stirring desire to depart from tradition, try Lemon Tofu "Cheesecake," Creamy Vanilla Frozen Dessert, Oranges with Dried Cherries and many other desserts that make delicious and delightful holiday endings.

Of course, if you can't decide on just one recipe, serving two or more desserts is a fantastic way to finish the big dinner with a flourish. When it comes to Thanksgiving dessert, it is perfectly acceptable to say "The more, the merrier!"

Winter Pudding

Oh, the English. They call all desserts "puddings." This is a cold winter version of a traditional English dessert called "summer pudding" made of fresh berries and bread. Top with a small scoop of fat-free sorbet or low-fat frozen yogurt.

MAKES 10 SERVINGS
(5 CUPS)

$^1/_2$ cup dried cranberries
$^1/_2$ cup dried currants
$^1/_2$ cup golden raisins
1 cup dried apricots, snipped into quarters
$^1/_2$ cup pitted prunes, snipped into quarters
5 cups water
1 teaspoon vanilla
3 to 4 tablespoons brown sugar, packed
$^1/_2$ teaspoon cinnamon
$^1/_2$ pound French or Italian bread, crust removed, sliced $^1/_2$ inch thick

In a large nonreactive saucepan, combine fruits and water; bring to a boil. Reduce heat to medium; simmer, uncovered, until fruits are tender, about 20 minutes. Add vanilla, sugar to taste and cinnamon. Cover; let steep 10 minutes.

Lightly oil bottom of a 7- or 8-inch-diameter nonreactive mold or glass bowl. Ladle enough juice from fruit mixture to cover bottom. Lay down bread slices to form a layer, tearing or cutting small pieces to fill in gaps. Ladle ⅓ fruit mixture over bread. Repeat process with bread and fruit for 2 more layers (3 bread layers in all), ending with fruit.

Lay plastic wrap over last layer of fruit. Top with a plate that fits inside mold or bowl. Weight plate with canned goods. Refrigerate, covered, 12 hours or overnight. Set mold or bowl in a larger bowl in case fruit juice drips over sides.

To serve, carefully loosen edges with a spatula or knife. Place a serving plate on top of mold or bowl. Invert pudding onto plate. Cut into wedges.

Per Serving: 171 Calories; 3g Protein; 1g Fat; 39g Carbohydrates; 0mg Cholesterol; 142mg Sodium; 4g Fiber.

Lemon Tofu "Cheesecake"

If you make this "cheesecake" the day before serving, its flavor will be more developed. (Plus, you don't have to worry about it while you're concentrating on those things that have to be made Thanksgiving Day.)

MAKES 8 SERVINGS

CRUST
2 cups graham cracker crumbs
$\frac{1}{4}$ cup maple syrup
$\frac{1}{4}$ teaspoon almond extract

FILLING
1 pound Japanese-style firm silken tofu
$\frac{1}{3}$ cup sugar
1 tablespoon tahini or almond butter
$\frac{1}{2}$ teaspoon salt
1 to 2 tablespoons fresh lemon juice
$\frac{1}{2}$ teaspoon lemon zest
$\frac{1}{2}$ teaspoon almond extract
2 tablespoons cornstarch dissolved in 2 tablespoons soymilk or rice milk

Preheat oven to 350°F. To make the crust, in a medium bowl, mix cracker crumbs, syrup and extract until crumbs are moistened. Pour into an oiled 9-inch pie plate; press mixture evenly to form crust. Bake 5 minutes; let cool while preparing filling.

To prepare the filling, blend all ingredients in a food processor or blender until smooth, about 30 seconds.

Pour mixture into crust. Bake until top of pie is slightly browned, about 30 minutes. Cool and refrigerate until thoroughly chilled and firm, about 2 hours.

VARIATIONS:

- *Use a prepared graham cracker crust.*

- *For a no-bake cheesecake, omit cornstarch mixture. Pour filling into crust and refrigerate until firm, at least two hours or overnight. The texture will resemble that of a cream pie.*

Per Serving: 212 Calories; 7g Protein; 5g Fat; 36g Carbohydrates; 0mg Cholesterol; 372mg Sodium; 1g Fiber.

Vegan Pumpkin Pie

The pie filling in this recipe needs to set overnight in the refrigerator, so make it the day before you serve it.

MAKES 8 SERVINGS

CRUST
½ cup unbleached flour
7 tablespoons whole-wheat pastry flour, plus additional flour for rolling
½ teaspoon salt
½ teaspoon sugar or granulated sugar cane syrup
½ teaspoon baking powder
3 tablespoons canola oil
3 tablespoons soymilk plus ½ teaspoon lemon juice, or buttermilk
3 to 4 tablespoons water

FILLING
2 cups canned pumpkin or pureed home-cooked fresh pumpkin (see Note)
1 cup low-fat soymilk, rice milk or low-fat milk
½ cup honey or ¾ cup granulated sugar cane syrup
¼ cup cornstarch
½ tablespoon dark molasses, or to taste
1 teaspoon vanilla extract
1 teaspoon ground cinnamon
½ teaspoon salt
½ teaspoon ground ginger
¼ teaspoon freshly grated nutmeg
¼ teaspoon ground allspice

To make the crust, in a medium bowl, combine flours, salt, sugar and baking powder. In a small bowl, mix oil and soymilk mixture or buttermilk.

Pour liquid mixture into dry ingredients and mix with a fork until dough holds together in a ball. If it is too dry, add some water, a little at a time, until dough is moist enough to roll. (If time allows, cover with plastic wrap and refrigerate for 1 hour.)

Roll out dough on a lightly floured surface with a lightly floured rolling pin, forming an 11-inch circle. Line a 9-inch pie plate with the dough. Flute or crimp the edges with your fingers or a fork. Cover with plastic wrap and refrigerate until ready to use.

Preheat oven to 425°F. To prepare the filling, in a large bowl, mix all remaining ingredients until smooth and blended. Pour into prepared crust and smooth top. Bake 10 minutes.

Reduce oven temperature to 350°F; bake until filling is set, about 50 minutes. Set on a wire rack to cool, then refrigerate overnight. Top with your choice of dessert topping, if desired.

NOTE: *If you are going to use fresh pumpkin for this pie, do not use the jack-o'-lantern type; the flesh of these large pumpkins is too watery and stringy. Instead, look for small pumpkins, sometimes called pie pumpkins, or other varieties of winter squash. To bake, cut pumpkins in half and remove seeds. Set, cut side down, in a lightly oiled baking pan. Bake at 400°F for 30 to 40 minutes. Scoop out the cooked flesh and puree.*

Per Serving: 280 Calories; 3g Protein; 6g Fat; 53g Carbohydrates; 0mg Cholesterol; 358 Mg Sodium; 3g Fiber.

Apple-Cranberry Crumb Tart

A delectable variation on apple pie, this tart also can be made with pears or peaches. Whatever fruit you use, it's sure to become a holiday favorite. The rolled oats in the crumb topping give the dessert extra crunch.

MAKES 10 SERVINGS

CRUST
1½ cups unbleached flour
Pinch salt
1½ tablespoons brown sugar
6 tablespoons butter, chilled
3 tablespoons cold water

FILLING
4 medium tart apples, such as Granny Smith, peeled and sliced ¼ inch thick
¾ cup fresh cranberries, rinsed
3 tablespoons unbleached flour
⅔ cup granulated sugar
½ teaspoon ground cinnamon

TOPPING
½ cup rolled oats
6 tablespoons unbleached flour
⅓ cup packed light brown sugar
3 tablespoons butter, melted

To make the crust, in a food processor, combine flour, salt and brown sugar. Process 30 seconds. With machine running, add butter through feed tube, then add water and continue processing until dough forms a ball, about 20 seconds. Wrap dough in plastic and chill at least 30 minutes.

Preheat oven to 375°F. Using your fingers, press dough into bottom and sides of a 10-inch tart pan with removable bottom. Cover and refrigerate until ready to use.

To prepare the filling, in a large bowl, toss apples and cranberries with flour. Stir in sugar and cinnamon. Spoon filling into pastry shell.

To make the topping, in a medium bowl, combine oats, flour and brown sugar. Add butter; crumble mixture with fingers. Sprinkle topping mixture over apples.

Bake until topping is golden and apples are tender, about 40 minutes. Transfer to a wire rack to cool. Remove side of pan, slice into wedges and serve.

Per Serving: 190 Calories; 1g Protein; 10g Fat; 23g Carbohydrates; 10mg Cholesterol; 147mg Sodium; 2g Fiber.

Ginger-Poached Pears in Red Wine

Poaching is a simple but excellent way to prepare pears, particularly if they are too hard to eat raw. Here, the pears are simmered in red wine, which imparts a rosy blush to the fruit and makes it a stunningly colorful dessert to serve. These pears are good served either hot or cold and will keep in the refrigerator for at least 24 hours.

MAKES 8 SERVINGS

8 ripe, firm medium pears, such as Bosc or Bartlett
1 cup fresh orange juice
2½ cups dry red wine
½ cup sugar
2 pieces preserved ginger, finely chopped
Thin strips orange peel for garnish

Peel pears, leaving stems on and removing as little flesh as possible. Take a thin slice off bottom to make a stable base. In a large saucepan, combine orange juice and wine. Add pears and simmer gently until tender, about 30 minutes.

Transfer pears to a shallow bowl or individual serving bowls. Add sugar and ginger to liquid in pan. Bring to a boil and simmer until syrupy, about 5 minutes. Spoon syrup over pears and garnish with strips of orange peel. Serve warm or chilled.

Per Serving: 220 Calories; 1g Protein; 1g Fat; 44g Carbohydrates; 0mg Cholesterol; 1mg Sodium; 1g Fiber.

Indian Pudding

Native Americans cooked cornmeal to a creamy porridge, then stirred in nut butter and maple syrup, honey or dried fruit.

MAKES 5 SERVINGS

2/3 cup yellow cornmeal
1/2 teaspoon ground ginger
1/4 teaspoon ground nutmeg
1/4 teaspoon salt
4 cups milk or soymilk, divided
1/3 cup maple syrup
2 tablespoons peanut butter or cashew butter
2/3 cups raisins or dried currants

Preheat oven to 275°F. Spray a 1½-quart casserole with vegetable cooking spray. Set aside. Sift together cornmeal, ginger, nutmeg and salt. Set aside. In a 2-quart saucepan, bring 3 cups milk or soymilk just to a boil over medium heat. Whisk in maple syrup. Gradually whisk in cornmeal mixture. Reduce heat to low. Cook 10 minutes, stirring frequently, until mixture is thick and smooth. Whisk in peanut butter or cashew butter. Stir in raisins or currants. Transfer cornmeal mixture to prepared dish. Pour remaining 1 cup milk or soymilk over top of mixture. Bake 2½ hours, until milk is absorbed and top of pudding is browned. Serve warm.

Per Serving: 407 Calories; 12g Protein; 13g Fat; 65g Carbohydrates; 33mg Cholesterol; 316mg Sodium; 3g Fiber.

Mince "Meat" Pie

Here's a recipe tailor-made for early preparation. The pie filling can be made ahead and refrigerated for up to 1 week before baking; the crust can be frozen or refrigerated for up to 2 weeks.

MAKES 8 SERVINGS

FILLING
1 unpeeled orange (see Note)
1 unpeeled lemon (see Note)
$1/2$ cup apple juice
2 large yellow apples, peeled, cored and diced
$3/4$ cup dark raisins, coarsely chopped
$1/2$ cup yellow raisins, coarsely chopped
$1/2$ cup brown sugar
$1/4$ teaspoon salt
$1/4$ teaspoon ground cinnamon
$1/4$ teaspoon ground cloves
$1/8$ teaspoon freshly grated nutmeg
1 teaspoon vanilla

CRUST
$1^1/2$ cups all-purpose flour
$1/8$ teaspoon salt
$1^1/2$ tablespoons light brown sugar
6 tablespoons soy margarine or butter
3 to 4 tablespoons cold water

To make the filling, roughly chop orange and lemon, including rinds. Discard seeds. Process with apple juice in a food processor fitted with a metal blade. Transfer to a large saucepan and add remaining filling ingredients except vanilla. Cover, and cook over low heat 25 minutes. Raise heat to medium and continue cooking 15 more minutes, stirring occasionally. Remove from heat. Gently stir in vanilla and allow mixture to cool.

To make the crust, combine flour, salt and brown sugar in a food processor. Process 1 minute using a standard cutting blade. Add margarine or butter and process 30 seconds more. Add water through the feed tube and allow dough to form into a ball. (Or, stir together flour, salt and sugar in a bowl. Cut in margarine or butter, and distribute evenly using a fork or your fingers. Add water, stirring to form a ball.) Wrap dough in plastic wrap and chill at least 30 minutes. Preheat oven to 350°F. Roll out dough with a rolling pin and place in a 9-inch pie pan. Make sure the dough along the sides of the pan is $1/4$ inch thick. Crimp edges and spoon in filling.

Bake 45 minutes. Serve warm or at room temperature.

NOTE: *Since you'll be eating the citrus peels, try to use organically grown fruit.*

🍂 Per Serving: 326 Calories; 4g Protein; 7g Fat; 63g Carbohydrates; 0mg Cholesterol; 230mg Sodium; 3g Fiber.

Tofu-Pumpkin Pie

This tasty version of a classic Thanksgiving dessert is egg- and dairy-free. Candied ginger adds a special festive touch.

MAKES 10 SERVINGS

CRUST
2 cups all-purpose flour
$^1/_2$ cup margarine or butter
1 teaspoon salt
3 to 4 tablespoons cold water

FILLING
1 pound firm tofu
19-ounce can pumpkin
1 teaspoon ground cinnamon
$^1/_4$ teaspoon freshly grated nutmeg
$^1/_2$ teaspoon salt
1 teaspoon vanilla
$^3/_4$ cup light brown sugar
$^1/_2$ teaspoon ground cloves
$^1/_3$ cup safflower oil
5 tablespoons candied ginger, chopped (or 1 teaspoon ground ginger)

To make the crust, combine flour, margarine or butter and salt in a food processor. Process for 30 seconds using a standard cutting blade. Add water through the feed tube and allow dough to form into a ball. (Or, stir together flour and salt in a bowl. Cut in margarine or butter, and distribute evenly using a fork or your fingers. Add water, stirring to form a ball.) Wrap dough in plastic wrap or wax paper and chill at least 30 minutes. Then roll out dough with a rolling pin and place in a 10-inch tart pan. Set aside.

Preheat oven to 350°F. To make the filling, combine all filling ingredients except candied ginger in a food processor or blender. (If using ground ginger, add it at this time.) Process until smooth, about 3 minutes. Add 3 tablespoons candied ginger, and process 30 seconds more. Pour filling into crust and bake 1 hour. Allow to cool.

HAPPY ENDINGS: DELICIOUS DESSERTS

Place remaining 2 tablespoons candied ginger in food processor or blender and process until coarsely ground. Sprinkle over top of pie. Serve warm or chilled.

HELPFUL HINT: *You may use an 8- or 9-inch pie pan instead of a 10-inch tart pan. Pour excess filling into custard cups and bake about 30 minutes until set.*

▰ Per Serving: 477 Calories; 10g Protein; 21g Fat; 66g Carbohydrates; 0mg Cholesterol; 387mg Sodium; 3g Fiber.

Spiced Pumpkin Custard

Want to serve your guests a lighter dessert? Instead of a high-fat pie, serve this low-fat pumpkin custard.

MAKES 8 SERVINGS

$^3/_4$ cup pumpkin puree (canned or fresh)
1 tablespoon honey
1 tablespoon molasses
$^2/_3$ cup maple syrup
2 to 3 tablespoons ground cinnamon
1 teaspoon ground ginger
$^1/_2$ teaspoon ground cloves
1 teaspoon ground nutmeg
$2^3/_4$ cups skim milk
2 tablespoons arrowroot powder or cornstarch
4 eggs, beaten (or 2 tablespoon Egg Replacer and $^1/_2$ cup water)
1 cup nonfat vanilla yogurt

Preheat oven to 350°F. Lightly oil eight 1-cup soufflé or custard dishes and place on a baking sheet. In a large, heavy-bottomed saucepan, combine pumpkin, honey, molasses, maple syrup, cinnamon, ginger, cloves and nutmeg. Mix ¼ cup milk in a small bowl with arrowroot or cornstarch. Add remaining 2½ cups milk, then pour milk and cornstarch mixture into saucepan. Stir well to combine with pumpkin mixture. Bring to a boil over medium heat, whisking frequently; cook until thickened to the consistency of heavy cream. Remove from heat. Stir in beaten eggs or Egg Replacer and water. Pour into baking dishes.

Bake 30 minutes, or until solid. Let cool slightly, then serve with a dollop of yogurt.

▰ Per Serving: 203 Calories; 8g Protein; 3g Fat; 38g Carbohydrates; 108mg Cholesterol; 101mg Sodium; 2g Fiber.

Pumpkin Freeze

This easy-to-make "ice cream" can be prepared several days ahead of time. Store the frozen cubes in freezer bags until you're ready to serve. Serve with Cardamom-Oatmeal Wafers (recipe follows).

MAKES 4 SERVINGS

6 ripe but firm bananas, peeled and cut into pieces
$1/3$ cup maple syrup, honey, frozen apple juice concentrate, apricot jam
    or other sweetener
$1/2$ to 1 tablespoon pumpkin pie spice
2 cups pumpkin puree or canned pumpkin
2 tablespoons finely chopped candied ginger for garnish (optional)

In a food processor, combine bananas, sweetener and pumpkin pie spice; puree. Add pumpkin and pulse until blended. Spoon mixture into 3 to 4 ice-cube trays (mini-ice-cube trays work best) and freeze until solid.

About 10 minutes before serving, remove frozen cubes from tray and place in food processor bowl to thaw a bit. (If using large ice cubes, chop cubes before processing.) Process until creamy. Spoon into chilled dessert dishes and sprinkle with candied ginger if desired.

Per Serving: 228 Calories; 3g Protein; 1g Fat; 58g Carbohydrates; 0mg Cholesterol; 10mg Sodium; 6g Fiber.

Cardamom-Oatmeal Wafers

Don't let the crumbly dough put you off: These cookies will hold together when cool.

MAKES ABOUT 54 WAFERS

1 cup sifted whole-wheat pastry flour
$\frac{1}{2}$ cup granulated sugar cane juice or brown sugar
$\frac{1}{2}$ cup rolled oats
1 teaspoon crushed cardamom seeds, or 1 tablespoon pureed fresh ginger root
    or candied ginger
$\frac{1}{2}$ teaspoon cream of tartar
$\frac{1}{4}$ teaspoon baking soda
$\frac{1}{4}$ teaspoon mace
3 tablespoons diced chilled unsalted butter or soy margarine
1 ounce semisweet chocolate, melted, for garnish (optional)

Preheat oven to 350°F. Spray an 8-by-11-inch or 9-by-12-inch baking dish with cooking spray.

Combine all ingredients except butter or margarine and chocolate in a food processor. Pulse to mix and pulverize oats. Add butter or margarine and process until mixture is crumbly. Sprinkle evenly into baking dish. With the back of a large spatula or with your fingers, press dough evenly and firmly into dish.

Bake until golden, 17 to 20 minutes. Cut into 1¼-inch squares while hot. Cool in pan on rack. To garnish, drizzle melted chocolate over cookies.

Per Wafer: 25 Calories; 1g Protein; 1g Fat; 4g Carbohydrates; 2mg Cholesterol; 6mg Sodium; 0g Fiber.

Corn Apple Cobbler

Corn, given to the Pilgrims by Native Americans, is central to the Thanksgiving experience. The bourbon in this recipe—corn in another form—is optional.

MAKES 8 SERVINGS
(ABOUT 6 CUPS)

1 quart fresh corn kernels
1 quart peeled, diced Granny Smith apples (about 4 medium)
$^1/_2$ cup sugar
$^1/_2$ cup brown sugar
3 tablespoons cornstarch
1 teaspoon cinnamon
2 tablespoons bourbon (optional)

TOPPING
$^3/_4$ cup unbleached all-purpose flour
$^3/_4$ cup cornmeal
1 tablespoon baking powder
5 tablespoons sugar
$^1/_2$ teaspoon salt
$^1/_4$ cup butter or margarine
$^1/_2$ cup reconstituted nonfat dry milk or rice milk
2 teaspoons vanilla

In a large bowl, combine corn, apples, sugars, cornstarch, cinnamon and bourbon (if desired), tossing to mix. Let stand.

To prepare topping, in bowl mix flour, cornmeal, baking powder, sugar and salt. Cut in butter or margarine until mixture is crumbly. Add milk or rice milk and vanilla, stirring with a fork to mix.

Place apple-corn mixture in a 9-by-13-inch baking pan. Drop topping by spoonfuls onto mixture. Bake until topping is golden and corn mixture is bubbling, about 35 minutes.

Serve warm in shallow bowls, topped if desired with vanilla ice cream, frozen yogurt or soy ice cream.

Per Serving: 392 Calories; 5g Protein; 7g Fat; 82g Carbohydrates; 16mg Cholesterol; 379mg Sodium; 5g Fiber.

Oranges with Dried Cherries

Orange-blossom water is available in Middle Eastern and gourmet specialty shops.

MAKES 6 SERVINGS

5 large navel oranges
2 teaspoons sugar or Sucanat
$1/2$ teaspoon cinnamon
2 teaspoons orange-blossom water
$1/2$ cup dried tart cherries
$1/4$ cup toasted chopped almonds
Fresh mint leaves for garnish

With a knife, peel skin and white pith from oranges. Place a strainer over a bowl; section oranges between membranes so there is nothing left but orange flesh. Excess juice should drip away from oranges. Place orange sections in dry bowl; add remaining ingredients except mint and toss lightly to mix. Garnish with mint.

Per Serving: 139 Calories; 2g Protein; 3g Fat; 28g Carbohydrates; 0mg Cholesterol; 2mg Sodium; 5g Fiber.

Maple Syrup Baked Apples

As with most very simple dishes, success depends on the quality of the ingredients. Use only the most flavorful apples, crack the walnuts yourself and use pure maple syrup.

MAKES 8 SERVINGS

8 large apples, peeled if desired and cored
1 cup maple syrup
1 cup chopped walnut meats

Preheat oven to 350°F. Place apples in a baking dish. Pour syrup over apples; sprinkle with walnuts. Bake 35 minutes.

Per Serving: 265 Calories; 4g Protein; 9g Fat; 46g Carbohydrates; 0mg Cholesterol; 4mg Sodium; 3g Fiber.

Cranberry-Orange-Pear Freeform Pie

Freeform pies aren't difficult to make, yet they look like they required a whole day in the kitchen.

MAKES 8 SERVINGS

1 recipe Yeasted Pastry Dough (recipe follows)
4 large, firm pears, peeled, cored and thinly sliced
$2\frac{1}{2}$ cups fresh cranberries
Juice and grated zest of 1 medium orange
$\frac{1}{4}$ teaspoon salt
$\frac{1}{4}$ teaspoon ground ginger
$\frac{1}{4}$ teaspoon freshly grated nutmeg
$\frac{3}{4}$ cup frozen pear or apple juice concentrate, thawed
2 tablespoons cornstarch
2 tablespoons frozen apple juice concentrate, thawed, for brushing

Prepare yeasted pastry. Preheat oven to 350°F. In a large bowl, mix pears, cranberries, orange juice and zest, salt, ginger and nutmeg.

In a small saucepan, combine juice concentrate and cornstarch. Stir constantly over medium-high heat until thick and smooth. Pour over pear mixture; combine thoroughly.

On a lightly floured surface, roll out yeasted pastry into a 16-inch circle. Carefully transfer dough to a greased cookie sheet or pizza pan. Pile pear filling in center of dough and bring edges of dough up around filling. Pleat edges, leaving about a 5-inch circle of fruit showing. Cover hole (not pastry) with a piece of foil cut to fit. Bake pie about 25 minutes, then brush pastry with apple juice concentrate. Bake 5 more minutes, or until golden brown.

Remove foil and serve hot or cooled with a frozen dessert or whipped topping.

Per Serving: 216 Calories; 4g Protein; 1g Fat; 50g Carbohydrates; 0mg Cholesterol; 165mg Sodium; 5g Fiber.

Yeasted Pastry Dough

This yeasted pastry uses mashed potatoes and soymilk—not fat—to make it tender. It works well with any juicy fruit filling, or with soft savory fillings.

Makes 8 servings
(1 free-form pie crust, 16 inches across)

½ cup warm soymilk
3 tablespoons leftover mashed potatoes or 3 tablespoons instant mashed
    potato flakes mixed with 2½ tablespoons hot water
1 tablespoon maple syrup or honey
1 teaspoon regular dry yeast or ½ teaspoon instant yeast
¼ teaspoon salt
¼ cup whole-wheat flour (not pastry flour)
1 cup unbleached flour, plus additional flour for kneading

Mix together soymilk, potatoes, syrup or honey and yeast in a medium bowl or a food processor bowl. Let stand 5 minutes. Add salt and flours. If using a food processor, process 30 seconds. Otherwise, mix and knead mixture on a lightly floured surface 5 minutes.

Place dough in an oiled bowl, oil top lightly, cover and let rise until doubled, about 1 hour. (You can also let dough rise in refrigerator from 2 to 24 hours.)

🍃 Per Serving: 98 Calories; 3g Protein; 1g Fat; 20g Carbohydrates; 0mg Cholesterol; 85mg Sodium; 1g Fiber.

Creamy Vanilla Frozen Dessert

For pie à la mode, try these recipes for vegan vanilla frozen dessert and vegan whipped topping.

MAKES 7 SERVINGS
(3½ CUPS)

1 cup water
¾ teaspoon agar powder or 1½ tablespoons agar flakes
⅓ cup honey, or ½ cup turbinado sugar or granulated sugar cane juice
10½-ounce package firm or extra-firm silken tofu, regular or low-fat
¾ cup low-fat soymilk or rice milk
½ tablespoon vanilla extract
¼ teaspoon salt

In a small saucepan, mix together water and agar. Stir over medium-high heat until it starts to simmer, then simmer 3 minutes. Pour into a blender with remaining ingredients; blend until very smooth. Freeze according to ice-cream maker directions. Let soften at room temperature before serving.

VARIATION: *Alternatively, freeze in ice-cube trays or in a flat pan. Cut frozen mixture into chunks and process in a food processor just before serving.*

Per Serving: 89 Calories; 4g Protein; 1g Fat; 16g Carbohydrates; 0mg Cholesterol; 124mg Sodium; 0g Fiber.

Silken Tofu Whipped Topping

10½-ounce package extra-firm or firm silken tofu, regular or low-fat
2 to 4 tablespoons sweetener of your choice
2 tablespoons fresh lemon juice
¼ teaspoon vanilla extract
⅛ teaspoon salt
⅛ teaspoon almond extract
Soymilk as needed

Place all ingredients in a blender or food processor; process until very smooth. Add soymilk a teaspoon at a time if mixture is too thick to blend well. Place in a covered container; refrigerate until chilled.

 Per Serving: 46 Calories; 3g Protein; 1g Fat; 7g Carbohydrates; 0mg Cholesterol; 69mg Sodium; 0g Fiber.

Orange Gingerbread

The orange in this gingerbread recipe gives this familiar holiday treat a kick.

$^1/_3$ cup canola oil, plus additional oil for greasing pan
1 cup dark molasses
$1^1/_4$ cups fresh orange juice
1 tablespoon finely grated orange rind
$2^1/_2$ cups whole-wheat flour
1 teaspoon baking soda
1 teaspoon cinnamon
2 teaspoons ground ginger
$^1/_2$ teaspoon salt
$^1/_2$ cup raisins

Preheat oven to 350°F. In a large bowl, mix together wet ingredients. In a medium bowl, sift together dry ingredients. Add raisins.

Add dry ingredients to wet ingredients and mix well. Pour into a greased 9-by-13-inch pan and bake 40 minutes, making sure not to overbake. Gingerbread will be moist.

Per Serving: 120 Calories; 2g Protein; 3g Fat; 22g Carbohydrates; 0mg Cholesterol; 107mg Sodium; 2g Fiber.

French Apple Cake

This dessert goes especially well with a warm cup of chai.

MAKES 12 SERVINGS

CAKE
2 pounds tart apples, cored, peeled and chopped (5 to 6 cups)
1 teaspoon ground cinnamon
$\frac{1}{2}$ teaspoon ground cloves
2 cups whole-wheat pastry flour
2 teaspoons baking powder
$\frac{1}{2}$ cup sugar
1 tablespoon maple syrup
$\frac{1}{4}$ cup milk
$\frac{1}{4}$ cup melted, cooled butter
4 large eggs, slightly beaten

TOPPING
4 large egg whites, slightly beaten
$\frac{1}{4}$ cup melted, cooled butter
$\frac{1}{2}$ cup packed light brown sugar
1 tablespoon almond extract
$\frac{1}{4}$ cup sliced almonds

To make the cake, preheat oven to 325°F. Grease a 9-by-13-inch baking pan. Toss apples with cinnamon and cloves. Spread evenly into prepared pan.

In a large bowl, mix flour, baking powder and sugar. Stir in syrup, milk, butter and eggs: Beat 90 seconds with an electric mixer on medium speed. Pour batter over apples. Bake until golden brown, about 45 minutes.

To make the topping, in a medium bowl, mix topping ingredients except almonds until blended. Spoon mixture over cake just as it comes out of oven. Sprinkle almonds over topping, return cake to oven and bake until topping is brown and bubbly, 10 to 15 minutes. Remove to a wire rack to cool. Serve warm or at room temperature.

Per Serving: 309 Calories; 5g Protein; 13g Fat; 45g Carbohydrates; 93mg Cholesterol; 177mg Sodium; 2g Fiber.

Fresh Pumpkin Pie

For cooking, buy small sugar pie pumpkins.

MAKES 8 SERVINGS
(ONE 9-INCH DEEP-DISH PIE OF 8 SLICES)

1¾ cups Fresh Pumpkin Puree (recipe follows)
¾ cup sugar
1½ teaspoon pumpkin pie spice
½ teaspoon salt
1½ cups evaporated skimmed milk
3 eggs, beaten
Unbaked 9-inch deep-dish pie crust

Preheat oven to 425°F. In a large bowl combine all ingredients except pie crust, stirring to mix well. Pour mixture into pie shell.

Place in oven 10 minutes. Reduce temperature to 350°F. Bake until a knife inserted in center comes out clean, about 40 to 50 minutes.

HELPFUL HINT: *To measure the capacity of pie plates, fill measuring cup with water and pour water into pie plate to the rim. Count the cups to determine the capacity.*

 Per Serving: 268 Calories; 8g Protein; 10g Fat; 38g Carbohydrates; 81mg Cholesterol; 347mg Sodium; 1g Fiber.

HAPPY ENDINGS: DELICIOUS DESSERTS

Fresh Pumpkin Puree

Once you taste the difference fresh pumpkin makes, you'll never go back to canned. Use this in recipes calling for pumpkin puree or canned pumkin.

MAKES 4 CUPS

1 small sugar pie pumpkin, 7 to 8 pounds seeded, cut into quarters

Preheat oven to 375°F. Bake pumpkin, cut sides down, in a baking pan until tender, about 1½ hours.

Remove from oven. Cool; scrape out pulp into bowl. Mash with a potato masher, then puree in batches in a food processor until smooth.

HELPFUL HINT: *Freeze unused puree in self-sealing freezer bags for later use.*

Per Cup: 49 Calories; 2g Protein; 0g Fat; 12g Carbohydrates; 0mg Cholesterol; 2mg Sodium; 2g Fiber.

LET'S FEAST:
Thanksgiving Dinner Menus

Menu 1

CREAM OF YAM AND CARROT SOUP

WARM SPINACH SALAD WITH CRANBERRY DRESSING

SWEET RICE, BUTTERNUT SQUASH AND GINGER

GREEN BEANS WITH MUSHROOMS MARSALA

CORN SAUTÉED WITH MINT AND SHIITAKE MUSHROOMS

PUMPKIN BREAD OR PUMPKIN-SPICE MUFFINS

WINE SUGGESTION: AN ASSERTIVE WHITE WINE SUCH AS RIESLING
OR GEWÜRZTRAMINER WILL GO WELL WITH THE MEAL'S SHARP FLAVORS
OF GINGER, CRANBERRY AND MINT, WHICH DEMAND A SPICY WINE.

Menu 2

AVOCADO DIP

ROASTED ASPARAGUS SALAD

AUTUMN RISOTTO WITH SQUASH AND SPINACH

BAKED CANDIED SWEET POTATOES

BRAISED LEEKS AND MUSHROOMS

BLUE CORN MUFFINS WITH CRANBERRIES

FRESH PUMPKIN PIE; FRESH PUMPKIN PUREE

WINE SUGGESTION: SELECT A NICE CHARDONNAY TO
COMPLEMENT THE CREAMY RISOTTO.

Menu 3

APPLE-CHEDDAR MUFFINS

POTATO-PUMPKIN SOUP

WILD AND BROWN RICE WITH LEEKS, ASPARAGUS AND CORN

SPINACH WITH PINE NUTS AND RAISINS

CRANBERRY-ORANGE-PECAN RELISH

CINNAMON-GLAZED CARROTS

LEMON TOFU "CHEESECAKE"

WINE SUGGESTION: HERE, A FRUITY WHITE ZINFANDEL WILL PAIR UP
NICELY WITH THE FRUITY RELISH, THE CINAMMON-GLAZED CARROTS AND THE
RAISINS IN THE SPINACH DISH. ON THE OTHER HAND, A DRY RED OR WHITE TABLE
WINE WILL MATCH THE MEAL'S EARTHY FLAVORS OF WILD AND BROWN RICE,
LEEKS AND PUMPKIN. IF YOU KNOW YOUR GUESTS' TASTES WELL ENOUGH,
CHOOSE A WINE BASED UPON THAT. IF NOT, MAKE BOTH AVAILABLE.

Menu 4

WOULD-YOU-LIKE-A-BITE STUFFED PORTOBELLO MUSHROOMS

CHESTNUT SOUP WITH GREENS

ACORN SQUASH TORTELLINI OR HERB AND WALNUT RAVIOLI

CHUNKY TOMATO GRAVY

BROCCOLI BAKE

CARROTS ON CARROTS

ZUCCHINI CORNBREAD

APPLE-CRANBERRY CRUMB TART

WINE SUGGESTION: THE TOMATO GRAVY DEMANDS A ROBUST RED WINE SUCH
AS BURGUNDY, MERLOT OR CABERNET SAUVIGNON.

Menu 5

Greens with Tangerine-Ginger Vinaigrette

Anasazi Bean Soup

Ken's Blue Cornbread

Vegetable Quinoa Bake with Red Kuri Squash

Zuni Succotash

Spinach with Pine Nuts and Raisins

Indian Pudding

Orange Gingerbread

Wine suggestion: The quinoa bake will have a mild nutty, herby flavor; a semi-dry white wine such as sauvignon blanc or Chablis will work here.

Menu 6

Apple-Walnut Salad with Watercress

Baked Pumpkin with Vegetable Pilaf

Sweet Potato Stuffing

Mushroom Gravy or Rich Mushroom Sauce

String Beans with Julienned Vegetables

Corn Sautéed with Mint and Shiitake Mushrooms

Cranberry-Port Relish

French Apple Cake

Wine suggestion: There is a strong, woodsy mushroom flavor in this menu, plus a grand pumpkin centerpiece stuffed with pilaf. Go with a red zinfandel or pinot noir, and if there is room, you can add a dry Riesling or chardonnay.

Menu 7

AZTEC PLATTER

MUSHROOM SOUP

CHEROKEE KANUCHI STEW WITH ROOT VEGETABLES

WILD RICE PILAF

DRIED CRANBERRY SAUCE

BROCCOLI BAKE

BOSTON MOLASSES MUFFINS

TOFU-PUMPKIN PIE

WINE SUGGESTION: THIS MENU COULD BE PAIRED WITH EITHER RED OR WHITE WINE. THE CRANBERRY SAUCE WILL BE TART AND FRUITY, AND THE PILAF AND SOUP WILL BE WOODSY. A DRY RED WINE SUCH AS A CABERNET SAUVIGNON OR RED ZINFANDEL WOULD BE A NICE SELECTION. IF WHITE WINE IS THE PREFERENCE, CHOOSE A DRY CHARDONNAY.

Menu 8

CREAM OF CORN SOUP

CAROL'S SEITAN ROAST WITH MUSHROOM GRAVY

STUFFED THANKSGIVING PUMPKINS

WILD RICE PILAF

CRANBERRY-ORANGE-PECAN RELISH

FLUFFY MASHED SWEET POTATOES

ZUCCHINI CORNBREAD

GINGER POACHED PEARS IN RED WINE

WINE SUGGESTION: THE SEITAN ROAST WITH GRAVY HAS A STRONG, SERIOUS FLAVOR. SERVE A DRY RED TABLE WINE.

Menu 9

Spinach-Cheese Twists

Pumpkin Soup

Succotash-Stuffed Butternut Squash

Cinnamon-Glazed Carrots

Honey-Glazed Onions

Mashed Garlic Potatoes Champ

Mushroom Gravy

Maple Syrup Baked Apples

Creamy Vanilla Frozen Dessert

Wine suggestion: The succotash-stuffed squash, carrots, onions and mushroom gravy all have an autumn-vegetable personality. Choose a nice white table wine such as Chablis.

Menu 10

Avocado Dip

Toasted Corn Salad with Citrus Vinaigrette

Harvest Vegetable Pie

Paprika Mashed Potatoes

Bulgur-Almond Stuffing

String Beans with Julienned Vegetables

Pumpkin-Apricot Quick Bread

Lemon Tofu "Cheesecake"

Wine suggestion: The flavors here are nutty bulgur, almonds and harvest vegtables. A white zinfandel, semi-dry Riesling or fruity blush wine would complement this menu nicely.

Menu 11

Autumn Tomato Bruschetta

Classic Onion Soup

Buttercup Squash, Parsnip and Cranberry Bean Stew

Hartzie's Cranberry Mold

Wild Rice with Dried Fruit

Green Beans with Mushroom Marsala

Four-Grain Cornbread

Maple Syrup Baked Apples

Creamy Vanilla Frozen Dessert

Wine suggestion: Serve a pinot noir or red zinfandel to balance the earthy and fruity elements of the menu.

Menu 12

Corn-Olive Salad

Vegetable–Wild Rice Soup

Shiitake Pot Pie with Polenta Crust

Royal Risotto with Asparagus and Artichokes

Fluffy Mashed Sweet Potatoes

Cinnamon-Glazed Carrots; Tofu Pumpkin Pie or Vegan Pumpkin Pie

Silken Tofu Whipped Topping

Wine suggestion: Here, pot pie and risotto will go well with a chardonnay or sauvignon blanc.

INDEX

Acorn Squash Tortellini, 74.
   See also Winter Squash
Anasazi Bean Soup, 50
Appetizers, 9–27
   Autumn Tomato Bruschetta,
     22
   Avocado Dip, 11
   Creamy Herb Spread, 23
   Endive Spears, 15
   Herbed White Bean Pâté, 26
   Lentil–and–Feta Loaf with
     Sun–Dried Tomato Catsup,
     24
   Marinated Mushrooms and
     Hazelnuts, 27
   Mixed Olives with Herbs, 17
   Mock Meatballs, 12
   Mushroom Crostini, 21
   Orange–and–Gold Millet
     Terrine, 18
   Roasted Garlic Cheese Rounds
     with Warm Tomato Sauce,
     13–14
   Spinach–Cheese Twists,
     19–20
   Stuffed Mushrooms, 16, 25
   Walnut–Stuffed Baby Red
     Potatoes, 20
   Would–You–Like–a–Bite
     Stuffed Portobello Mushroom,
     25
Apple
   Brandy, 32
   Cake, 210
   –Cheddar Muffins, 177
   Cobbler, 203

Cocktail, 32
–Cranberry Crumb Tart, 195
Focaccia, 163–164
Maple Syrup Baked, 204
Muffins, Candied, 185
Potato–Mushroom Soup with,
   41
Pumpkin Curry with, 97
Salad, Simple–but–Symbolic,
   59
Sauce, Ginger, 144
–Walnut Salad with Watercress,
   65
Artichokes, Royal Risotto with,
   115
Asparagus
   Roll–Ups, 56
   Royal Risotto with, 115
   Salad, 60
   Wild and Brown Rice with,
     96
Autumn Tomato Bruschetta, 22
Avocado Dip, 11
Aztec Platter, 55

Baked
   Apples, 204
   Candied Sweet Potatoes, 118
   Pumpkin with Vegetable
     Pilaf, 95
   Stuffed Onions, 125
   Sweet Potatoes and Red
     Potatoes, 139
   Sweet Potatoes with
     Yogurt–Rice Topping, 145
Balsamic Dressing, 62

Basic
   Bread Dough, 159–160
   Vegetable Stock, 135–136
Beans
   Anasazi Bean Soup, 50
   Black–Eyed Pea, Corn and
     Sweet Potato Salad, 57
   Corn, Sweet Potato and Green
     Bean Salad, 61
   15–Bean and Winter Squash
     Chili, 89
   Herbed White Bean Pâté, 26
   Salad, 55
   Stew, Butternut Squash,
     Parsnip and Cranberry, 99
Beets, Posole Casserole with,
   92–93
Beverages, 29–35
   Apple Brandy, 32
   Apple Cocktail, 32
   Café Latte, 33
   Chai Masala, 34
   "Champagne," 33
   Mock Champagne, 31
   Rosy Mulled Cider, 31
Biscuits
   Easy Drop, 166
   Half–Wheat, 167
Black–Eyed Pea, Corn and Sweet
   Potato Salad, 57
Blue Corn
   Bread, 165
   Muffins with Cranberries,
     170
Boston
   Brown Bread, 186–187

Molasses Muffins, 178
Braised
    Leeks and Mushrooms, 138
    Seitan Roll with Apricots and
        Turnips, 83–84
Bread, 157–187
    Apple Focaccia, 163–164
    Basic Bread Dough, 159–160
    Boston Brown, 186–187
    Corn Batter, 169
    Four–Grain Corn, 171
    Garlic–Herb, 162
    Ken's Blue Corn, 165
    Pumpkin, 184–185
    Pumpkin–Apricot Quick, 183
    Super Grain Corn, 173
    Sweet Potato Corn, 182
    White Wheat, 168–169
    Zucchini Corn, 172
Breadsticks, 175
Broccoli Bake, 119
Brown Gravy, 153
Bruschetta, Autumn Tomato, 22
Bulgur
    –Almond Stuffing, 140
    Mock Meatballs, 12
Butternut Squash
    Parsnip and Cranberry Bean
        Stew, 99
    Risotto with, 93
    Succotash–Stuffed, 98
    Sweet Rice and, 107
    Tarts, 90

Cabbage in Red Wine, 122
Café Latte, 33
Cake
    French Apple, 210
    Lemon Tofu "Cheesecake," 192
Candied
    Apple Muffins, 185
    Sweet Potatoes, 118
Cardamom–Oatmeal Wafers, 202
Carol's Seitan Roast with
        Mushroom Gravy, 79
Carrots
    Cinnamon–Glazed, 132
    Cream of Yam and Carrot Soup,
        39

and Leek Tortellacci, 75
on Carrots, 136
Orange–and–Gold Millet
    Terrine, 18
Sweet Potato and Spiced Fruits,
    131
Catsup, Sun–Dried Tomato, 25
Celery Root and Potatoes, Mashed,
    146
Chai Masala, 34
Champ, Mashed Garlic Potatoes,
    120
"Champagne," 31
    Mock, 31
Cheese
    Cake, Lemon Tofu, 192
    Rounds with Roasted Garlic,
        13–14
    Stuffed Endive Spears, 15
    Twists, Spinach, 18–19
Cherokee Kanuchi Stew with Root
    Vegetables, 103
Chestnut
    and Corn Patties, 179
    Soup with Greens, 44
    Stuffing, 73–74
Chili, 15–Bean and Winter Squash,
    89
Chou à la Bourguignonne, 122
Chowder, Mushroom Wild Rice, 47
Chunky Tomato Gravy, 151
Cider, Rosy Mulled, 31
Cinnamon–Glazed Carrots, 132
Citrus Vinaigrette, 64–65
Classic Onion Soup, 45
Cobbler, Corn Apple, 203
Cookies, Cardamon–Oatmeal, 202
Corn
    Apple Cobbler, 203
    Aztec Salad, 55
    Black–Eyed Pea, and Sweet
        Potato Salad with, 57
    Chestnut and Corn Patties, 179
    Muffins with Cranberries, 170
    –Olive Salad, 63
    Salad with Citrus Vinaigrette,
        64–65
    Sautéed with Mint and Shiitake
        Mushrooms, 124
    See also Succotash

Soup, Cream of, 42
Sticks, 181
Sweet Potato and Green Bean
    Salad, 61
Wild and Brown Rice with, 96
Cornbread
    Batter Bread, 169
    Four–Grain, 171
    Ken's Blue, 165
    Super Grain, 173
    Sweet Potato, 182
    Zucchini, 172
Cornmeal
    Crust, Posole Casserole with,
        92–93
    Indian Pudding, 197
Cranberry
    Bean Stew with, 99
    Blue Corn Muffins with, 170
    Dressing, Warm Spinach Salad
        with, 54
    Mold, Hartzie's, 139
    –Orange–Pear Freeform Pie,
        205
    –Orange–Pecan Relish, 121
    –Port Relish, 117
    Sauce, 91
Cream of
    Corn Soup, 42
    Yam and Carrot Soup, 39
Creamy
    Herb Spread, 23
    Vanilla Frozen Dessert, 207
Crostini, Mushroom, 21
Curry, Pumpkin with Lentils and
    Apples, 97
Custard, Spiced Pumpkin, 200

Desserts, 189–212
    Apple–Cranberry Crumb Tart,
        195
    Cardamom–Oatmeal Wafers,
        202
    Corn Apple Cobbler, 203
    Cranberry–Orange–Pear
        Freeform Pie, 205
    Creamy Vanilla Frozen Dessert,
        207
    French Apple Cake, 210
    Fresh Pumpkin Pie, 211

Ginger–Poached Pears in Red
  Wine, 196
Indian Pudding, 197
Lemon Tofu "Cheesecake,"
  192
Mince "Meat" Pie, 198–199
Oranges with Dried Cherries,
  204
Pumpkin Freeze, 201
Spiced Pumpkin Custard, 200
Tofu–Pumpkin Pie, 199–200
Vegan Pumpkin Pie, 193–194
Winter Pudding, 191
Dinner Rolls, 160
Dip, Avocado, 11
Dried
  Cherries, Oranges with, 204
  Cranberry Sauce, 91
  Fruit, Wild Rice with, 128
Drinks. See Beverages
Drop Biscuits, 166

Easy Drop Biscuits, 166
Endive Spears, 15
Entrees, 67–109
  Acorn Squash Tortellini, 74
  Baked Pumpkin with Vegetable
    Pilaf, 95
  Braised Seitan Roll with
    Apricots and Turnips, 83–84
  Butternut Squash, Parsnip and
    Cranberry Bean Stew, 99
  Butternut Squash Tarts, 90
  Carol's Seitan Roast with
    Mushroom Gravy, 79
  Carrot and Leek Tortellacci, 75
  Cherokee Kanuchi Stew with
    Root Vegetables, 103
  15–Bean and Winter Squash
    Chili, 89
  Golden Lentil Roulade with
    Chestnut Stuffing, 73–74
  Green Rice with Winter
    Squash, 71
  Harvest Vegetable Pie, 84–86
  Herb and Walnut Ravioli, 76
  Layered Seitan Vegetable
    Dinner, 69
  Millet Loaf with Mushroom
    Sauce, 108

Mushroom Bourguignonne in a
  Whole Pumpkin, 78–79
Mushroom–Pecan Stew, 104
Pattypan Squash Stuffed with
  Split Peas, 72
Posole Casserole with Beets,
  Sweet Potatoes and Cornmeal
  Crust, 92–93
Pumpkin Curry with Lentils
  and Apples, 97
Shiitake Pot Pie with Polenta
  Crust, 102–103
Spinach Roulade, 80–81
Succotash–Stuffed Butternut
  Squash, 98
Sweet Rice, Butternut Squash
  and Ginger, 107
Vegetable Pancakes with
  Roasted Plum Sauce, 70
Vegetable Quinoa Bake with
  Red Kuri Squash, 94
Vegetable Tagine with Olives
  and Prunes, 100–101
Vegetarian Shepherd's Pie,
  105–106
Vegetarian Tourtiére, 87–88
Wild and Brown Rice with
  Leeks, Asparagus and Corn,
  96

Fast Pizza Dough, 176
15–Bean and Winter Squash Chili,
  89
Fluffy Mashed Sweet Potatoes, 127
Focaccia, Apple, 163–164
Four–Grain Cornbread, 171
French Apple Cake, 210
Fresh
  Pasta Dough, 77–78
  Pumpkin Pie, 211
  Pumpkin Puree, 212
Frozen Dessert
  Creamy Vanilla, 207
  Pumpkin, 201

Garlic
  Cheese Rounds with Warm
    Tomato Sauce, 13–14
  –Herb Bread, 162
  Potatoes, Mashed, 120

Ginger
  Applesauce, 144
  Bread, 209
  Dressing, 116
  –Poached Pears in Red Wine,
    196
Glazed Shallots and Walnuts, 123
Goat cheese stuffed, Endive
  Spears, 15
Golden Lentil Roulade with
  Chestnut Stuffing, 73–74
Gravy, 149–156
  Brown, 153
  Chunky Tomato, 151
  Mushroom, 152
  Mushroom–Walnut, 155
  See also Sauce
Green Beans
  Corn and Sweet Potato Salad,
    61
  with Mushrooms Marsala,
    133
Green Rice with Winter Squash,
  71
Greens
  Chestnut Soup with, 44
  with Tangerine–Ginger
    Vinaigrette, 53
  See also Salads
Guest vegetarians, 7–8

Half–Wheat Biscuits, 167
Hartzie's Cranberry Mold, 139
Harvest Vegetable Pie, 84–86
Hazelnuts and Mushrooms,
  Marinated, 27
Herb
  Spread, Creamy, 23
  and Walnut Ravioli, 76
  White Bean Pâté, 26
Honey–Glazed Onions, 126
Hosting tips, 1–8
Hot Corn Sticks, 181

Indian Pudding, 197

Kanuchi Stew with Root
  Vegetables, 103
Ken's Blue Cornbread, 165

Layered Seitan Vegetable Dinner, 69
Leeks
   and Carrot Tortellacci, 75
   and Mushrooms, Braised, 138
   Wild and Brown Rice with, 96
Lemon
   Tofu "Cheesecake," 192
   Vinaigrette, 59
Lentil
   —and—Feta Loaf with
      Sun—Dried Tomato Catsup, 24
   Pumpkin Curry with, 97
   Roulade with Chestnut
      Stuffing, 73–74
Loaves
   Lentil—and—Feta with
      Sun—Dried Tomato Catsup, 24
   Millet with Mushroom Sauce, 108

Manners, 7–8
Maple Syrup Baked Apples, 204
Marinated Mushrooms and
   Hazelnuts, 27
Mashed Celery Root and Potatoes, 146
Mashed Potatoes
   Garlic Champ, 120
   Paprika, 137
   Perfect, 113
   Soy, 114
Mashed Sweet Potatoes, 127
   with Parsnips and Carrots, 130
Menus, 212–218
Mexican—style Cheese Rounds, 14
Milk, steaming, 35
Millet
   Loaf with Mushroom Sauce, 108
   Terrine, Orange—and—Gold, 18
Mince "Meat" Pie, 198–199
Mixed Olives with Herbs, 17
Mock
   Champagne, 31
   Meatballs, 12
Molasses Muffins, 178
Muffins
   Apple—Cheddar, 177

Blue Corn with Cranberries, 170
Boston Molasses, 178
Candied Apple, 185
Orange—Oat, 161
Pumpkin—Spice, 174
Mulled Cider, Rosy, 31
Mushrooms
   Bourguignonne in a Whole
      Pumpkin, 78–79
   Braised Leeks and, 138
   Corn Sautéed with, 124
   Crostini, 21
   Gravy, 152
   and Hazelnuts, Marinated, 27
   Marsala, Green Beans with, 133
   Medley, 114
   —Pecan Stew, 104
   Potato Soup with Apple and, 41
   Sauce, 109, 154, 156
   Shiitake Pot Pie with Polenta
      Crust, 102–103
   Soup or Sauce, 49
   Stuffed, 16, 25
   —Walnut Gravy, 155
   Wild Rice Chowder, 47

Oatmeal Wafers, Cardamom, 202
Olives
   —Corn Salad, 63
   with Herbs, 17
Onions
   Baked Stuffed, 125
   Honey—Glazed, 126
   Soup, Classic, 45
Orange
   with Dried Cherries, 204
   Gingerbread, 209
   —and—Gold Millet Terrine, 18
   —Oat Muffins, 161
   —Glazed Snow Peas, 123–124
   Vinegar, 53

Pâté, Herbed White Bean, 26
Pancakes
   Sweet Potato, 180
   Vegetable Pancakes with
      Roasted Plum Sauce, 70
Paprika Mashed Potatoes, 137

Parsnip and Sweet Potato
   Casserole, 134
Pasta Dough, 77–78
Pastry Dough, 206
Patties, Chestnut and Corn, 179
Pattypan Squash Stuffed with Split
   Peas, 72
Pears
   Ginger—Poached in Red Wine, 196
   Salad in Raspberry Vinaigrette, 58
Pecan—Mushroom Stew, 104
Peppers
   Red Pepper Sauce, 82
   Roasted Red Pepper and Sweet
      Potato Soup, 40
Perfect Mashed Potatoes, 113
Pie
   Cranberry—Orange—Pear
      Freeform, 205
   Fresh Pumpkin, 211
   Harvest Vegetable, 84–86
   Mince "Meat," 198–199
   Shiitake Pot Pie with Polenta
      Crust, 102–103
   Tofu—Pumpkin, 199–200
   Vegan Pumpkin, 193–194
   Vegetarian Shepherd's, 105–106
   Vegetarian Tourtiére, 87–88
Pilaf with Ginger Dressing, 116
Pizza Dough, 176
Planning tips, 3–4
Plum Sauce, 70
Polenta Crust, 102–103
Portobello Mushroom,
   Would—You—Like—a—Bite
      Stuffed, 25
Posole Casserole with Beets, Sweet
   Potatoes and Cornmeal Crust, 92–93
Potatoes
   Baked Sweet and Red, 139
   Mashed Celery Root and, 146
   Mashed Garlic Champ, 120
   —Mushroom Soup with Apple, 41
   Paprika Mashed, 137
   Perfect Mashed, 113
   —Pumpkin Soup, 46
   Soy Mashed, 114

Walnut–Stuffed Baby Red, 20
See also Sweet Potatoes
Preparation tips, 4–5
Presentation tips, 6
Pudding
    Indian, 197
    Winter, 191
Pumpkin
    –Apricot Quick Bread, 183
    Baked with Vegetable Pilaf, 95
    Bean Stew with, 99
    Bread, 184–185
    Curry with Lentils and Apples,
        97
    Custard, Spiced, 200
    Freeze, 201
    Mushroom Bourguignonne in,
        78–79
    Pie, 193–194, 211
    –Potato Soup, 46
    Puree, 212
    Soup, 48
    –Spice Muffins, 174
    Stuffed, 142
    –Tofu Pie, 199–200
Puree, Fresh Pumpkin, 212

Quinoa
    Bake, 94
    –Corn Salad, 55
    Super Grain Cornbread, 173

Raspberry Vinaigrette, 58
Ravioli, Herb and Walnut, 76
Red Kuri Squash, Vegetable Quinoa
    Bake with, 94
Red Pepper
    Roasted, and Sweet Potato
        Soup, 40
    Sauce, 82
Relish
    Cranberry–Orange–Pecan, 121
    Cranberry–Port, 117
Rice
    Butternut Squash and Ginger,
        107
    with Leeks, Asparagus and
        Corn, 96
    with Winter Squash, 71
    See also Risotto
Rich Mushroom Sauce, 154

Risotto
    with Asparagus and Artichokes,
        115
    with Squash and Spinach, 93
Roasted
    Asparagus Salad, 60
    Garlic Cheese Rounds with
        Warm Tomato Sauce, 13–14
    Plum Sauce, 70
    Red Pepper and Sweet Potato
        Soup, 40
Rolls, Dinner, 160
Root Vegetables
    Cherokee Kanuchi Stew with,
        103
    Thyme–Roasted, 117
Rosy Mulled Cider, 31
Roulade
    Golden Lentil with Chestnut
        Stuffing, 73–74
    Spinach, 80–81
Royal Risotto with Asparagus and
    Artichokes, 115

Salad, 51–65
    Apple–Walnut with Watercress,
        65
    Asparagus Roll–Ups, 56
    Aztec Platter, 55
    Black–Eyed Pea, Corn and
        Sweet Potato, 57
    Corn, Sweet Potato and Green
        Bean, 61
    Corn–Olive, 63
    Greens with Tangerine–Ginger
        Vinaigrette, 53
    Roasted Asparagus, 60
    Simple–but–Symbolic Apple, 59
    Toasted Corn with Citrus
        Vinaigrette, 64–65
    Warm Spinach with Cranberry
        Dressing, 54
    Winter Pear in Raspberry
        Vinaigrette, 58
Sauce, 149–156
    Brown Gravy, 153
    Chunky Tomato Gravy, 151
    Dried Cranberry, 91
    Mushroom Gravy, 152
    Mushroom, 49, 109, 156

Mushroom–Walnut Gravy, 155
    Red Pepper, 82
    Rich Mushroom, 154
    Roasted Plum, 70
    Warm Tomato, 14
Seitan
    Roast with Mushroom Gravy,
        79
    Roll with Apricots and Turnips,
        83–84
    Vegetable Dinner, 69
Shallots and Walnuts, Glazed, 123
Shepherd's Pie, Vegetarian,
        105–106
Shiitake
    Mushrooms, Corn Sautéed
        with, 124
    Pot Pie with Polenta Crust,
        102–103
Side dishes, 111–147
    Baked Candied Sweet Potatoes,
        118
    Baked Stuffed Onions, 125
    Baked Sweet Potatoes and Red
        Potatoes, 139
    Baked Sweet Potatoes with
        Yogurt–Rice Topping, 145
    Braised Leeks and Mushrooms,
        138
    Broccoli Bake, 119
    Bulgur–Almond Stuffing, 140
    Carrots on Carrots, 136
    Chou à la Bourguignonne, 122
    Cinnamon–Glazed Carrots,
        132
    Corn Sautéed with Mint and
        Shiitake Mushrooms, 124
    Cranberry–Orange–Pecan
        Relish, 121
    Cranberry–Port Relish, 117
    Fluffy Mashed Sweet Potatoes,
        127
    Ginger Applesauce, 144
    Glazed Shallots and Walnuts,
        123
    Green Beans with Mushrooms
        Marsala, 133
    Hartzie's Cranberry Mold, 139
    Honey–Glazed Onions, 126
    Mashed Celery Root and
        Potatoes, 146

Mashed Garlic Potatoes
  Champ, 120
Mashed Sweet Potatoes with
  Parsnips and Carrots, 130
Mushroom Medley, 114
Orange–Glazed Snow Peas,
  123–124
Paprika Mashed Potatoes, 137
Perfect Mashed Potatoes, 113
Royal Risotto with Asparagus
  and Artichokes, 115
Soy Mashed Potatoes, 114
Spinach with Pine Nuts and
  Raisins, 143
String Beans with Julienned
  Vegetables, 129
Stuffed Thanksgiving
  Pumpkins, 142
Sweet Potato, Carrots and
  Spiced Fruits, 131
Sweet Potato and Parsnip
  Casserole, 134
Sweet Potato Stuffing, 147
Thyme–Roasted Root
  Vegetables, 117
Wild Rice and Apricot Stuffing,
  141
Wild Rice with Dried Fruit,
  128
Wild Rice Pilaf with Ginger
  Dressing, 116
Zuni Succotash, 127
Silken Tofu Whipped Topping,
  208
Simple–but–Symbolic Apple Salad,
  59
Snow Peas, Orange–Glazed,
  123–124
Soup, 37–50
  Anasazi Bean, 50
  Basic Vegetable Stock, 135–136
  Chestnut with Greens, 44
  Classic Onion, 45
  Cream of Corn, 42
  Cream of Yam and Carrot, 39
  Mushroom, 49
  Mushroom Wild Rice Chowder,
    47
  Potato–Mushroom with Apple,
    41
  Potato–Pumpkin, 46
  Pumpkin, 48

Roasted Red Pepper and Sweet
  Potato, 40
Vegetable–Wild Rice, 43
Soy Mashed Potatoes, 114
Spiced
  Fruits, Sweet Potato and
    Carrots, 131
  Pumpkin Custard, 200
  tea (chai masala), 34
Spinach
  –Cheese Twists, 19–20
  with Pine Nuts and Raisins,
    143
  Risotto with, 93
  Roulade, 80–81
  Salad with Cranberry Dressing,
    54
Split Peas, Pattypan Squash Stuffed
  with, 72
Spreads, Creamy Herb, 23
Squash
  15–Bean and Winter Squash
    Chili, 89
  Green Rice with, 71
  Parsnip and Cranberry Bean
    Stew, 99
  Risotto with, 93
  Stuffed with Split Peas, 72
  Succotash–Stuffed, 98
  Sweet Rice and, 107
  Tarts, 90
  Vegetable Quinoa Bake with, 94
  Zucchini Cornbread, 172
String Beans with Julienned
  Vegetables, 129
Stuffed
  Mushrooms, 16, 25
  Thanksgiving Pumpkins, 142
Stuffing
  Bulgur–almond, 140
  Sweet Potato, 147
  Wild Rice and Apricot, 141
Succotash
  –Stuffed Butternut Squash, 98
  Zuni, 127
Sun–Dried Tomato Catsup, 25
Super Grain Cornbread, 173
Sweet Rice, Butternut Squash and
  Ginger, 107
Sweet Potatoes
  Baked, 139
  Baked Candied, 118

Black–Eyed Pea, Corn Salad
  with, 57
Cakes, 180
Carrots and Spiced Fruits, 131
Corn, and Green Bean Salad,
  61
Cornbread, 182
Fluffy Mashed, 127
Mashed with Parsnips and
  Carrots, 130
and Parsnip Casserole, 134
Posole Casserole with, 92–93
Roasted Red Pepper Soup with,
  40
Stuffing, 147
with Yogurt–Rice Topping, 145
See also Yams

Tagine with Olives and Prunes,
  100–101
Tangerine–Ginger Vinaigrette,
  Greens with, 53
Tart
  Apple–Cranberry Crumb, 195
  Butternut Squash, 90
Tea, spiced (chai masala), 34
Terrine, Orange–and–Gold Millet,
  18
Thyme–Roasted Root Vegetables,
  117
Toasted Corn Salad with Citrus
  Vinaigrette, 64–65
Tofu
  "Cheesecake," 192
  Creamy Vanilla Frozen Dessert,
    207
  –Pumpkin Pie, 199–200
  Whipped Topping, 208
Tomato
  Bruschetta, 22
  Gravy, Chunky, 151
  Sauce, warm, 14
  See also Sun–Dried Tomato
Tortellacci, Carrot and Leek, 75
Tortellini, Acorn Squash, 74
Tourtiére, Vegetarian, 87–88
Twists, Spinach–Cheese, 18–19

Vanilla Frozen Dessert, 207
Vegan Pumpkin Pie, 193–194
Vegetable
  Layered Seitan Dinner, 69

Pancakes with Roasted Plum
    Sauce, 70
Pie, 84–86
Pilaf, Baked Pumpkin with, 95
Quinoa Bake with Red Kuri
    Squash, 94
Stock, 135–136
Tagine with Olives and Prunes,
    100–101
–Wild Rice Soup, 43
See also specific vegetables
Vegetarian
    guests, 7–8
    Shepherd's Pie, 105–106
    Tourtiére, 87–88

Walnut
    –Apple Salad with Watercress,
    65

and Herb Ravioli, 76
–Stuffed Baby Red Potatoes, 20
Warm
    Spinach Salad with Cranberry
        Dressing, 54
    Tomato Sauce, 14
Watercress, Apple–Walnut Salad
    with, 65
Whipped Topping, Silken Tofu,
    208
White Bean Pâté, Herbed, 26
White Wheat Bread, 168–169
Wild Rice
    and Apricot Stuffing, 141
    and Brown Rice with Leeks,
        Asparagus and Corn, 96
    with Dried Fruit, 128
    Mushroom Chowder, 47
    Pilaf with Ginger Dressing, 116

Vegetable–Wild Rice Soup, 43
Wines, choosing, 29–30
Winter Squash
    Green Rice with, 71
    15–Bean Chili with, 89
    See also Acorn Squash
Winter
    Pear Salad in Raspberry
        Vinaigrette, 58
    Pudding, 191
Would–You–Like–a–Bite Stuffed
    Portobello Mushroom, 25

Yams, Cream of Carrot Soup with,
    39. See also Sweet Potatoes
Yeasted Pastry Dough, 206

Zucchini Cornbread, 172
Zuni Succotash, 127